ALIGNED &
Unstoppable

Praise for *Aligned and Unstoppable*

Once again Cass has created a masterpiece; a heartfelt, down-to-earth, relatable guide that encourages, inspires and empowers women to take a deep dive into their fears, to find their true self and their true purpose, own it, and lead their best life. Inspirational and practical, *Aligned and Unstoppable* provides the tools needed to reflect and develop, both personally and professionally, and reach your full potential.

Kate Callaghan, holistic nutritionist, wellness
speaker and author of *Holistic Nutrition*

Reading *Aligned and Unstoppable* brought me back into centre, into balance and into deep remembrance of my own gifts, purpose and light to share in this world, arriving at a time I teetered and wavered. If you're feeling lost, unsure or unclear about the next steps, this book will bring you back to your why (and why not) and reconnect you to the creative juices within. Another brilliant book from Cassie Mendoza-Jones!

Helen Jacobs, author of *You Already Know*

It has been with much anticipation that I have waited for a book that has the ability to truly light you up, inject hope and self-belief, and offer an unwavering sense of empowerment like *Aligned and Unstoppable* does. Cassie has a way with words that makes you feel like she's talking directly to your soul, and this book is no different. I can't wait for people all over the world to release the fears and limiting beliefs that are holding them back from their dreams, by devouring the pages of this book.

Jordanna Levin, author of *Make It Happen*

In all her writing, Cassie shines a light on the creative process and shows us how to trust ourselves as we create. In *Aligned and Unstoppable*, Cassie shares the steps of taking our creations out into the world. Reading it is like having a delicious cup of tea with a business maven.

Ali Walker, author of *Get Conscious*

I love reading everything Cass writes. I always feel like it's a chance to sit down with a wonderfully wise and funny best friend who really understands what you're going through. I love the insights I receive—thank you for reminding me to start where it feels big!—and the practical tips and tools she shares. Reading *Aligned and Unstoppable* will put you into exactly the space you need to be in to do your highest and best work in the world and to be visible in the process. What a gift!

Samantha Nolan-Smith, founder and CEO of
The School of Visibility

Aligned and Unstoppable is the straight-talking, tea-brewing companion every modern woman should have on hand. Laying her own failures, insecurities and successes on the table, Cassie will (gently) shake you unstuck and give you a (friendly) leg up towards your creative and business goals—or something even better.

Melanie Dimmitt, journalist and author of *Special*

Aligned and Unstoppable is not only inspirational, practical and relatable, but it also encourages and creates genuine self-acceptance and appreciation for wherever you are in your business or creativity journey. The practical tips and affirmations, in combination with Cassie's personal examples, make this book the perfect guide to inspire confidence and align you to your dreams, whatever they may be. Thank you for sharing Cassie, your words are truly special.

Belinda Kirkpatrick, naturopath and
author of *Healthy Hormones*

When I'm going round in circles, feeling a bit wobbly and unsure of what my next move should be in my business (or life!), I'll return to this book. It's the perfect roadmap to tune back in, and help you feel aligned and unstoppable. It helped me appreciate and feel immense gratitude in my life now, while joyfully and lightly holding a vision for the future. What a delicious book!

Amanda Rootsey, youth mentor, coach and
author of *Shine from Within*

ALSO BY CASSIE MENDOZA-JONES

You Are Enough
It's All Good

ALIGNED & Unstoppable

How to Align to Your Dreams, Clear Away
Fears and Call In What's Next

Cassie Mendoza-Jones

HAY HOUSE

Carlsbad, California • New York City
London • Sydney • New Delhi

Copyright © Cassie Mendoza-Jones, 2019

Published in the United States by: Hay House, Inc.: www.hayhouse.com®
Published in Australia by: Hay House Australia Pty. Ltd.: www.hayhouse.com.au
Published in the United Kingdom by: Hay House UK, Ltd.: www.hayhouse.co.uk
Published in India by: Hay House Publishers India: www.hayhouse.co.in

Design by Rhett Nacson
Cover design by Edie Swan Design
Typeset by Bookhouse, Sydney
Edited by Margie Tubbs
Author Photo by Bayleigh Vedelago

ISBN: 978-1-4019-6109-1
E-book ISBN: 978-1-4019-5980-7

10 9 8 7 6 5 4 3 2 1
1st Australian edition, January 2020
1st United States edition, April 2020

Printed in the United States of America

To my baby girl, Asher Mila.

May you know your worth, trust yourself,
and step confidently towards your dreams.

Dig inside yourself. Inside, there is a spring of goodness ready to gush at any moment, if you keep digging.

MARCUS AURELIUS, *MEDITATIONS*

Contents

Introduction

I was done, over it, on my way out.

I couldn't keep going the way I was: feeling stressed about my work; worrying about my path in life and business; questioning everything from my purpose to my career; not trusting myself enough; and wondering why (in my imagined conversations) it always seemed so much easier for everyone else.

I was ready to give up, to throw my hands in the air and say, 'I'm done!' (On that note, I had no idea what I'd do next. But where I stood felt too hard, and I wanted out of that.)

I decided to pull an oracle card, from a deck I'd almost given away just weeks before, but at the last minute, had decided to keep.

The card I pulled had one word on it: *Stay*.

Goosebumps

I stayed. And the idea for this book dropped in.

I'll tell you what this book isn't ...

— a story of rags to riches

— a story about an overnight success

— a story about how I made six figures in six months

Instead, this is a book about having the courage to use your voice and love what you create, in both life and work, no matter your situation.

This is a book that'll help you start doing the work you love, by really trusting yourself, honouring your voice, and speaking up; by letting yourself succeed and fail and rise and fall (and rise again) along the way.

This book is written for anyone who wants to become aligned to what they're truly wishing to call into their lives and work, and for those who want to deepen their self-belief and self-expression, to help them love what they create. It blends spirituality with practical tools, to help you build a beautiful, sustainable creative life, work and business that lights up your soul, and the world.

I want to help you give yourself permission to have an even clearer, stronger and more empowered voice, expressed by how you're showing up in your life, business and self-expression—and of course, how you're showing up in the world.

I've been working with women, entrepreneurs, healers, coaches and creatives for years. I know that working towards your dreams, using your voice, and building a beautiful, thriving life and business needs the inner work done first. And the right mindset means more than a big social media presence (no matter how many likes or shares a photo gets). The alignment that inner work creates does more for your dreams than chasing yourself into the ground, hustling straight to burnout.

My clients are naturopaths, nutritionists, psychologists, kinesiologists, copywriters, graphic designers, reiki and crystal healers, crystal store owners, writers, teachers, lecturers, painters, artists, interior designers, consultants, yoga teachers, massage therapists, beauty therapists, make-up artists, personal trainers, life coaches, health coaches, wedding stylists, PR and HR consultants, and more.

Whether they've been running their business for years, working in a corporate job while setting up a passion project on the side, balancing work for someone else while they work for themselves too, making a big change in their careers, leaving something old behind to start something new, or new mums coming back to work and setting up a business that serves their families even more deeply, I've seen how this works, in so many different ways. The first step is always deeply rooted in self-belief, and a desire to create a more deeply aligned life.

This inner work, this alignment work balanced with soulful strategy and self-belief, is the work I do all the time—in my own life and business, with my clients, and through my books, workshops, online programs and social media presence.

This book is about me and my creative life and work, and you and yours. I wrote it to help you align to your dreams, clear away fears, perfectionism and procrastination, and show up more fully in your life and business. It's about finding, honing and using your voice to light up the world.

I wrote it to help you succeed with joy and fail without fear, and to help you lean into—and trust—every single moment in between, and way beyond.

This book has been brewing under the surface for years. It's one I didn't always know I'd write, and one that I now can't wait to share with you. It's one I hope helps you remember (every day, even when you're uncertain, even when you're overwhelmed, even when you're feeling stuck) that you can always clear your blocks and become more aligned to what you're working towards and receiving. You can become unstoppable, in the best way possible—not the burn-outy, fatiguey version of unstoppable, but the magnetic, expansive, energised version.

This book is about honouring all the work we've already done, honouring ourselves for where we are and where we want to be, approaching everything we create from a space of self-worth, and extending that out into the world.

I wrote this book to help you begin trusting yourself even more; to help you know that you are enough in your creative life and business; to help you know your voice is needed; and to help you know your work is enough.

Becoming aligned and unstoppable is about releasing expectations and attachments, leaning into the unknown, releasing your fear of being seen and speaking out, showing up for yourself even when feeling unsure of the outcome, and trusting yourself—and your intuition—to help you build your best business and life, as well as honour your soul gifts.

Through this book, you'll uncover how to:
— Trust yourself, before anything else
— Adopt the best mindset, to support you in working towards your dreams and goals
— Begin loving what you create
— Align yourself to your most thriving life, work, career, path, purpose and business
— Back yourself and your work, no matter its form
— Embody and honour your soul work
— Sit down and do the work you know you're called to do
— Honour your soul-based gifts and deepen your purpose-based path, by listening to your intuition and not simply by stressing out about strategy

— Deepen your self-belief and self-confidence in what you're creating
— Pivot without fear of judgement, releasing the fear of judgement about what you're creating and how you're showing up in your life
— Use all your talents, so you can show up in the most aligned and expansive way possible (no more splitting yourself across several passions, but rather, combining your gifts to support your dreams)
— Release comparison in your life, work and business
— Realise your value, and then find (and hone) your unique voice
— Expand the energy of your business, and expand your body of work
— Cultivate your personal power, to help you work towards your dreams
— Allow yourself to receive and create an abundant mindset and energy, to help you build the life and biz you are worthy of
— Trust that 'good enough' is perfect (because it is)
— Do the inner work first, so the outer work becomes easier
— Trust yourself, where you are right now, and what you're working towards
— Set healthy energetic boundaries, to support your best self and best work
— Do less and take lots of brain holidays, because the world doesn't need the burnt out, exhausted version of you
— Create the best, most aligned business and life, always showing up for yourself in an authentic way
— And more ...

The chapters are split up into five parts relating to your thoughts and mindset, fears and blocks, expression and creativity, self-care, self-belief and more. But as you'll learn (and as I'm sure you already experience in your own life), it all overlaps.

If you're feeling shaky in your mindset and not honouring your creativity, then running your business or deepening your work, career or path might not be feeling fluid and expansive right now. If you're feeling unhealthy and ungrounded in your life, then showing up to teach and share with others won't feel great either.

While I do recommend reading this book from front to back the first time, after that you can pick up the book, flick open a page or turn to a random chapter and read as you need. As I've said in my previous books, I believe that if you turn to a random page right now, that page will contain something you need today, something to support you in this moment.

In and among everything, you'll find questions, journalling prompts, energetic clearing exercises, and more. I often end chapters with something you can do, say, think or visualise—perhaps an affirmation to work with, or something else you can take away and apply in your everyday life (like an energetic essence to take, or a crystal to work with). And lastly, the book ends with a balancing and activating meditation.

Everything in the following chapters has a 'take it or leave it' vibe. Take the advice if it resonates with you; leave it if it doesn't. If there's one thing I know about creativity, business, doing the work you love and honouring your dreams, it's that there is no one-size-fits-all approach, no cheat sheet, no done-for-you script, and no one way to do things.

There are many ways. For you, there's only your way—the way that feels best for you.

So find it, make it, create it and own it. And then? Do your absolute best work, take all the breaks you need, keep at it, and keep remembering that you've got this.

And finally:

— Get excited! A whole new world awaits you (and there's so much space for you).

— Invest in yourself; with time, abundance, compassion, self-determination, love and more.

— Take action. Through showing up for yourself and doing the work within these pages, you'll be empowered to take action and uplevel your creativity and self-belief throughout your life, business and work. What you do next is up to you.

— Be patient with yourself, your ever-evolving creativity and self-awareness, your ever-and-always-deepening soul-based gifts and purpose, and the Universe. Give yourself time to grow and learn. This won't happen overnight, but as you'll discover, you wouldn't want it to.

— Show up, as best you can and as often as you can (but also ... take lots of lovely breaks, please and thank you).

— Be brave and courageous.

— Let fear lead you sometimes (she's often showing you the way to go). But also be okay to put fear to bed, and show up fiercer and braver than ever before.

— Let resistance lead you; she's often testing you to see how much you want this.

— Don't let perfectionism get the best of you; by the end of this book, you'll crave the feeling of releasing what you create.

— Look after yourself first—before work, clients or business.

— Ask for support, and let yourself receive it.

— Grow before you feel ready (sometimes you'll need to).

- Have faith in yourself; in your growing creativity, self-confidence, voice, gifts, purpose and the Universe.
- And lastly ... trust yourself. A lot. Always. And then trust yourself some more.

Okay, let's get going. We have so much amazing work to do.

Part 1

———

THE INNER WORK
Thoughts and Mindset

CHAPTER 1

That Could Work ...

I was 24 years old when I started my business. (Nowadays, I joke that I didn't realise I was starting a business). I was fresh out of nutrition college. In fact, I'd been offered a job as the sole nutritionist in a multidisciplinary clinic a month before I graduated.

I'd been emailing clinics, looking for admin work while I was completing my nutrition studies. I was still studying some naturopathy subjects to add onto my accreditation, and thought that if I worked as a receptionist while I built up my client base on the side, that might be a nice way to ease into my new business.

But the Universe had other plans. I received a reply that said, 'We're not looking for receptionists, but would you like to be our nutritionist?'

Um, that could work.

I had a month between graduating and my first day in my new clinic. When I got to work that first day, 24 May 2011, I had no clients booked in. Not one. But I showed up anyway, because I was too excited not to. I believed that if I showed up and spent time in the clinic, even if I had no clients booked in, I'd be showing the Universe I was serious about this. I'd also use the time to take action to draw clients towards me. (And, I assumed, make a lot of tea in the meantime.)

As I was getting ready to leave for the day, my clinic director popped her head into my room. With a smile on her face, she said, 'Check your calendar.' A new client had booked in for that evening. My hubby had told someone in his office that I was working as a nutritionist, and she'd picked up the phone and made an appointment straightaway.

And just like that *snaps fingers* my business began.

Since that day, my business has evolved from nutrition and naturopathy to kinesiology, as well as life and business alignment coaching, writing and speaking. It has shifted from a wellness focus, to focusing on energy, emotions and creativity.

Now, the work I do blends personal and business development with energy alignment. Now, the work I do lights me up, more than ever before.

Nutrition and naturopathy were simply how my business began. Actually, not quite—this wasn't really the beginning of my creative career at all. As we'll go through soon, using our skills means we use all our skills ...

The rest of the story is how it evolved. The rest of the story is everything that came after my decision to begin a business, with no clients and a buzzing mix of anticipation, expansion and fear. The anticipation of starting something new, something I'd worked so hard to begin, and something I felt so drawn to.

The expansion ... that feeling of opening up to what's next, knowing this is exactly what your soul needs for its next level of growth.

And the fear ... of course, the fear! The fear of: 'But what if no-one wants to work with me? What if I'm terrible at this?

What if I put everything into it, and lose it all? What if this is an absolute failure? What if I am an absolute failure?'

But I did it anyway. Because, as we'll go through in these pages, feeling that fear—or worry, nervousness, overwhelm, perfectionism, procrastination or whatever else you're feeling—and doing it anyway, getting to the other side of it, is one of the best feelings in the world. It's the feeling I seek and search for, the one I bow in gratitude to, the one that makes me feel full and whole and on purpose, the one that whispers to me to keep going.

That feeling is how we grow. It's okay and normal and common to feel the fear. But what's not common is you, and your voice, and your gifts. And that's what you're asked to reveal when you show up for yourself, when you speak up, and when you move through the resistance that sometimes asks you to be quiet, or to quit, or to procrastinate, or to keep pushing things to the side.

Sure, there's always 'tomorrow'. But how would it feel if tomorrow you could work on speaking up again, instead of for the first time? What if every tomorrow were filled with you using your voice, sharing your gifts, and emptying yourself of your best work to fill yourself to the brim?

It doesn't matter where you've come from, because you're here now. And if you're here, it's because you know there's something (or many things) for you to make and create, share and release. It might be through your business, your career, your writing, or your art. It may simply—importantly—be through you, and your voice.

But no matter the vessel or vehicle of your voice, if you're here, it's time to tune into it and trust it. And to know that finally, and always, you've got this. It's your time. So, let's do this.

You're here now

It doesn't matter how many businesses you've started and not stayed in, how many art projects you've left unfinished, how many blog posts are sitting unpublished on your website, or how many times you've told yourself you can't.

It doesn't matter where you've come from, because you're here now. And now is the moment you decide what you'll tell yourself next.

You may have to change your inner talk more than once, but now is the moment you give yourself permission to forgive yourself for all the things you think you haven't done, or made, or created, or finished; for all the paths you think you should've trodden; for all the places you think you should already be.

Now is the time to recognise that all those loose ends, all that confusion about what to do next, all those unfinished blog posts or art projects or businesses were necessary for you to get you to this point, where you decide to start again; and this time, to show yourself you can.

Use that unfinished work, those not-quite-completed works of art, those barely laid paths, to fuel your future work. Let the bricks you didn't finish laying become the framework for the path you build going forwards. You are not a failure because you didn't finish something. Instead, how wonderful it is that you let go of something that wasn't feeling right to you.

From this point on, everything is possible

Years ago, when I was finding it really hard to find a happy weight, I went to see a naturopath (before I'd graduated as one myself). She told me something that can be applied to so many areas of our lives, and has stayed with me ever since. She told me that if I wanted to lose weight, I had to let go of my defeatist attitude; that when I believed I could lose weight, I'd be so much closer to making the changes that would allow that to happen. I had to change my thoughts, energy and mindset, before I could affect change in my reality. But if I stayed feeling stuck and defeated, then my attitude would reflect my results.

My first response to her saying this was: 'Yes, that sounds lovely, but I've tried all that before, and the reason I'm here is because that didn't work for me. It must be something else.'

Though even as I spoke those words, I realised that she was right. I had to change my thoughts, energy and mindset, before I could affect change in my reality.

So I invite you to do the same thing here, in relation to your writing, creativity and business; in relation to your path, purpose and gifts; in relation to whatever you're wishing to create and receive, dream up and call in. I ask you to leave your past 'failures' at the door, and see them as catalysts for your growth.

When we let ourselves start where we are, while also acknowledging what's come before this moment, we give ourselves the best possible chance to continue moving towards what we're wishing to create.

By staying stuck in the past, in the 'coulda, woulda, shoulda' vibes of resentment and regret, we continue to live out our past stories; we continue to tell ourselves that 'one day' things will change, but we don't take responsibility for starting to create the change from within, today.

Everything you've done has brought you to this point. From this point on, everything else is possible. Bravo to that!

JOURNALLING PROMPT

Think of three situations you've experienced that didn't quite go to (your) plan, and the reasons you're grateful you had them. Did they leave you in an unexpected but wonderful place? Did they teach you a hard but brilliant lesson? Did they help you move forwards in an even more aligned direction?

Grab your journal or a notebook (hey, even the Notes section in your phone will do, although there's something cathartic about putting pen to paper) and get writing.

Then, do this:

— Place your hands over your heart.

— Take a deep, calming, cleansing, grounding breath in.

— Say to yourself: *I'm in exactly the right place, today. I trust how I got here, and I trust that from here, everything else is possible. I know that I am deeply supported, as I take the next step forwards. So I lean into this support, creating what calls to me most, or something better.*

— Now, give yourself a hug (or a kiss, or a wink to your reflection, or a glass of prosecco) and keep moving forwards.

CHAPTER 2

Follow the Work that Lights You Up

It was a balmy evening in Santa Barbara, California. I'd arrived late the night before for a conference, having flown in for just five days, all the way from Sydney.

Arriving at the hotel, I dropped my suitcase off in my room and went down to the bar. I ordered a big glass of Californian red (deeeelicous) and looked around, soaking it all in. I felt like I was on top of the world I'd created for myself.

Next day, after wandering the sweet streets and visiting a favourite local coffee shop I'd frequented while on holiday with my hubby, Nic, just a few months prior, I went back to the gorgeous boutique hotel and took myself up to the rooftop pool. It had views across beautiful Santa Barbara, with mountains on one side and the ocean on the other. I took a deep breath in. I cracked open my notebook and started scribbling out scripts for chakra meditations, which I'd later record once I got home.

People who listen to those particular meditations (you'll know if you have) consistently comment on how much they love them. Apart from them resonating with my work, I have a theory about why.

Firstly, I believe it's because I wrote them in Santa Barbara on that beautiful warm afternoon, looking out at the mountains and the sea. Although I've only been twice, Santa Barbara feels like home to me in some way, and this definitely came through in my writing.

Secondly, I believe it's because I was following what lights me up. Writing those meditations on the rooftop, while travelling overseas to attend a conference for a software company I love was a new experience for me, and a memory I'll always cherish. Not only that, I'd never written a meditation album before, and I felt real excitement and expansion at the thought of doing so.

Along the way though, I had to ask myself (countless times): 'Can I do this work I love?' The answer, sitting on that rooftop, was a resounding, pounding 'Yes!'.

This is your invitation to join me. To do the work that lights you up; to do the work that lights the way for others to find their own light; to let yourself become aligned and unstoppable, on your path to loving what you create.

Trust yourself, before anything else

Pop quiz time (circle all the answers that apply). The best place to start is:

A. At the beginning
B. Exactly where you are right now
C. Kind of today, but also kind of somewhere far off into the future where 'one day' lives, where you're perfect, and everything is in its perfect place, and life went just to plan

C, right? Just kidding. It's A and B, and a beautiful combination of them.

For you to take action on any of the words that come through on these next pages, for you to receive anything you're wanting to create and trying to make space for, and for you to rise to where you want to be, you have to know already, right now, that you are enough.

When you know that you are enough, then by extension you know that your work is enough. And to release your work into the world, you have to trust yourself, even while you continue to explore and discover deeper layers of who you are.

Before you take a step forwards, you have to trust yourself, back yourself and believe in yourself.

This isn't arrogance I'm asking you to adopt, but rather a system of self-belief that you might not have taken on board before. I don't want you to run recklessly into your future, undermining yourself and your hard work by expecting things or thinking you deserve to be successful, simply because you're working hard.

On that note ... to shift out of a state of entitlement, we need to shift into showing up with more soul. This becomes easier and feels more natural, the more aligned to your truth you become.

So I invite you now, in this chapter and in every following chapter, to show up for yourself and your work, for your creativity and your voice, and for all the parts of you that want to be seen and heard, that want to create and share, celebrating yourself every step of the way.

As you'll discover, if you don't back yourself, how can you ask anyone else to?

So let's do that, first. Before anything else, trust yourself. You don't need some earth-shattering change to rumble through you for this to happen. You can decide, right now, that you and your voice, your work and your dreams—all of you—is enough.

From this space, you can do the work you know you came here to do. From this space, you can create, and share, and speak, and move towards your dreams.

From this space, you can ask others to join you on this journey, but only if you trust yourself (and your higher and deepest self) first.

'Why' and 'why not'

When we're working towards something (whether it's in our life, biz, career, or dreams we don't even fully understand yet), it's good to know our 'why'.

Our 'why' makes up part of our greater purpose, the reason we're feeling called to do what we do. Our 'why' might be related to something we've experienced and want to help others navigate, a deeper reason that drives a passion, a calling, or something that whispers to us and won't let us forget it. It's important to have an inkling—or a deep knowing—of what this is.

It's also important to think of your 'why not'. Your 'why not' is the part of you that can't not create, that can't not do this work, that can't not work towards what you're creating. Put more simply, it's the part of you that has to; the part that can't put that new spark of an idea to rest until you've lit the match and started to bring it into form.

Your 'why' isn't always the first reason for creating something in your life and business. You create it because you have to, because it calls for you and tugs at you, drawing you closer.

Your 'why not' might shift and change, but at its core it remains the same. The answer to your 'why not' is often as simple as: 'Because I have to ... because I can't not.'

Even if you don't know the outcome; even if you don't know all the details (yet); even if you can't see the bigger picture (yet);

even if the resistance feels like it's creating mountains out of molehills, and you feel far away from your dreams; even if creating it calls for you to change your mind, to stand up for something you believe in (that no-one else can see), to course-correct, and to back yourself more fully.

What is your 'why not'? What do you have to do, and create, and make, and share? What's calling your name? Will you answer the call?

Honour and trust what you love

Now that you've given yourself permission to trust yourself, to follow your 'why not', and to deepen your work, I invite you to believe in yourself and trust what you're creating.

You must believe in yourself first, if you are to invite others to believe in you too.

By this I mean that whatever your version of creativity and 'doing the work' and business looks like, whatever you're working on in your life, trust how it's showing up for you. Stop looking outside yourself and comparing your life and work to everyone else. Allow yourself to love what your work looks like, and how it's coming through for you.

Trusting yourself—your innate worth, your business/career acumen, your creativity, as well as your choices and decisions—is how you'll build a beautiful, sustainable business, a purposeful path, and a deeply creative and fulfilled life.

Love and accept your work

I love business; it's in my blood. Almost everyone in my family is an entrepreneur and has created a business and career they love.

So I grew up watching how business is done; I grew up knowing it's safe to create, honour and work towards a dream.

And yet it took me months to come to accept that this book would be about business, writing, spirituality, creativity and loving what you're creating in life and business.

I kept trying to talk myself out of writing a book about these topics, especially one relating to business and creativity, because I didn't want to alienate people who might get something out of my book, but who didn't run their own business. But underneath that was a tinge of fear—the fear of judgement. I wondered, 'Who am I to write this book?'

As I sat down to journal one morning, I asked my Guides a question through automatic writing. This is a way of journalling where you ask the Universe (or whatever higher power you believe in) a question, and then just let whatever answer flows through you land on the page. The answer I received was, *The whole book is already written.* (If there's ever a sentence that'll soothe a writer's soul, that's it!) I knew then that this book was to be the next step in my creative journey, the next piece to add to my body of work, fears and all.

Then I remembered something else: I deeply wanted to write this book. The idea had dropped in months ago, and the book had been coming through in sentences and phrases, words and themes, for months and months.

I realised that I had to do this for myself, first and foremost. I realised that by dimming my own light—ignoring what lights me up—I wasn't doing anyone any favours. (Especially when writing a book about doing the work that lights you up!)

I also remembered that my business and my writing are simply the vessels for my creativity. Perhaps in just one area of my life, but we each have many vessels we can funnel our fullest potential into.

You may be here because you run your own business (or want to one day); because you're a writer (or want to give yourself permission to say so); or because you want to start honing and using your unique voice to fully express and create in your life. Whatever the reason, I hope that by being here, you're reminded of your own light, and you answer a resounding 'yes' when asked if you'll show up more fully in your life, creativity and business.

To do this, you must first love and accept your work. By 'work', I mean whatever you're doing that lights you up the most, whatever work you can't imagine not doing. You must honour it, fully and deeply and in all the right places.

Don't worry about possible judgement coming from others, or from yourself. Don't let yourself dream up the worst possible scenarios about how your work will be revealed or received by others. Love and accept it for what it is, and for how it wants to come through you. Only then can you release it to others.

See your work as your personal power project; see what you create as the vessel for how you speak to the deepest parts of yourself. Then you'll always honour it, because you're honouring yourself.

JOURNALLING PROMPTS

— What are some of your 'why nots'? Write them down and keep them where you can see them daily.
— What do you need to give yourself permission to do/think/ feel/be?

— If you truly let yourself love and accept your work, what would feel different for you? What could change?

ALIGNED AND UNSTOPPABLE AFFIRMATION

I trust myself, my voice, and what I'm creating every day. I let myself deepen what I desire, stand up for what I believe, and do the work that lights me up.

CHAPTER 3

Dream Big but Start Small

Many of us go big, when we dream about our dreams. We see ourselves at the 'end' of our path, or years down the track; we see the vision we're brewing and drawing, mapping and sketching. We refine the details, we hold it close to our hearts and wish it would come true with all our might. We decide that this is how things should go.

But what we don't always do is remember that while it's wonderful to dream big, the way to get there is by starting small.

Starting small is about seeing the bigger vision and holding it in your sights, as you start carving out the path to get there. Starting small is about taking one step, and then another, so that when you look back you can see the path you've been carving out—the one that'll take you to your dreams (or something better).

You can't always map your path until you've walked it, but that doesn't mean you shouldn't start.

Mapping your path is about relinquishing fairytale notions about what it'll be like to work towards your dreams and goals, and doing the work with heart anyway. It's about feeling the overwhelm but recognising that it isn't a barrier to success. Just like fear, your overwhelm can show you that you're doing something big, something that you need to do.

Go big, but also trust and know that it's beautiful to go small.

All the small steps add up to the big, and the big is where your dreams lie. So start small; map it out in baby steps; dive deep into the overwhelm, so that clarity rises to the surface as you take deep breaths to guide you on your way. See your bigger picture in front of you (in baby steps) and behind you (in the path you've already trodden). Trust you'll get there, or somewhere better, all in good time.

Start where it feels big

Okay, in seemingly direct contradiction to what you've just read, this is where I invite you to start where it feels big. But the difference is that this is in relation to your deepest creative work.

I invite all my clients to do this, when they feel the pull to create something, to do something they've maybe never done before, but don't know where to begin. That's when I say, 'Start where it feels big.'

It feels big whenever it feels like you'll be doing your deepest work.

It feels big whenever it feels like this is what you came here to do, even if it terrifies you and lights you up in equal measure. (That's because you can feel expansion and fear at the same time.)

It feels big whenever you feel the most resistance—the resistance that says, 'You can't', to which you reply, 'Oh, but I can.'

Your biggest work is the work that calls to you in the silent moments in between; where lines you'll later write drop down into your consciousness; where words float through your mind and you grab onto them with your pen, inviting them to live with you on paper. It's the work that needs you, and only you, to call it through; to channel it, create it, and cultivate it through your words, your work, your energy, your intentions and your commitment to create.

If you start where it feels big, you'll do the important work first (even if that means starting small).

When you do the important work first, the little voice that says 'I can't' starts to fade. The more you start where it feels big, and the further into yourself and your creativity you roam, the more you'll hear the whispers of 'Oh, but I can', over and over until they transform, slowly but surely, into 'See? I could'.

What feels big to you?

For me, this writing project felt big. I think that's because this work is in the deepest part of me; it's what I've always known, explored within myself, and aimed to do through my work and self-expression. However, that doesn't mean it's always been easy to do. My first two books called on me to understand new parts of myself, through the experiences I went through when writing them. This book, however, simply (and overwhelmingly) called on me to embody what I already knew to be true; to deepen how I already live; to continue to clear away fears (and clear them away, and clear them away); to more fully commit to what I already create, write and believe; and then to help you to do the same.

So, what feels big to you? It's often where you feel the most resistance, but it can also be where you feel the most fear, the most joy, the most tension, or the strongest possibility.

When you start where it feels big, you get to lean into and use all of that fear, joy, tension or possibility. And then you create 'big', because you start where it matters most.

The little things that feel urgent can be a distraction. They are the molehills that feel like mountains, but they don't move you closer to your dreams. Whereas the mountain that's calling you won't recede into the distance, until you start climbing it.

If you can't start where it feels big or small, just start. In the words of author and entrepreneur, Seth Godin: *It's easy to fall so in love with the idea of starting that we never actually start.* So just sit down and do the work.

This morning, I bumped into a friend as I was getting coffee. He asked what I was up to, and I said I was diving back into writing this book, as I'd taken a long break from it.

'Sometimes that's good though, right?' he asked.

'Yes, it's very good, but I'm now ready to get back into it,' I replied. 'I've left it for long enough, and if I keep leaving it, nothing will change.'

The idea of starting can be intoxicating. It's like that feeling I used to love before a new school year started, when I'd go to the stationery shop with my mum, to buy new pencils, a pencil case, new notebooks and folders. The newness was intoxicating and irresistible (even though I also knew it really signalled a whole new year of school!).

Sometimes the newness and brainstorming and planning and energy of being 'nearly ready' can energise us; but it can also halt us. Sometimes we just have to dive in before we're ready. It's the only way we'll know if this new path is for us. It brings our dreams and desires out of the ether and into reality and practicality. It makes us intentional in our thoughts and actions: *How can I rise to meet this dream of mine?*

So, just start. Give yourself the chance so many people don't, because fear and smallness and insecurity and procrastination get in the way. Let your overwhelm be the catalyst that fuels you; let your perfectionism be a mirror, guiding you through what's not working, into what does.

JOURNALLING PROMPTS

— What's feeling big for you right now?
— What's holding you back from getting started?
— What's overwhelming you? Get it all down on paper; you'll see what matters, what doesn't, and what'll get done without you worrying about it.
— What do you need to do/say/release/take action on, in order to begin/continue/move forwards?

A VISUALISATION FOR CLARITY

Close your eyes; place one hand on your forehead (covering your Third Eye chakra, the space between eyebrows) and one hand over your heart space.

Take a deep breath in and out of your nose. Centre and ground your energy.

Visualise yourself taking one step in front of the other in the direction you wish to go, leaning into what feels like the next best step for you, trusting whatever guidance or insights drop in. Really feel into what this might look (or feel) like for you.

Spend another few moments here, and let any other guidance or inspiration drop in.

Open your eyes whenever you're ready, letting yourself feel more confident and capable, knowing you can start from exactly where you are.

ALIGNED AND UNSTOPPABLE AFFIRMATION

I let myself take one step in front of the other, in order to weave the path that's most aligned to me. I do the work that feels big; the work that calls to me the most; the work that won't let me forget it.

CHAPTER 4

Deep Belief and Light Attachment

When we have a strong drive and desire to honour our dreams, and to do the work that'll support us in reaching them, we can also become a little attached to them. We may start to believe that the only way to make our dreams come true is to hustle to burnout; or fight tooth and nail for them; or ignore everything else except our goals; or map them out exactly, so that nothing could possibly go wrong. (That's how it works, right?)

We think our plan is the 'only' plan. We stop believing in our internal compass of success and put all our eggs in one basket—that basket of belief that says our dreams can and will only come true if we focus single-mindedly on them. It's as if we're trying to control them, by focusing on the one way they can come true.

So what might happen, if those dreams you're dreaming about don't happen? What would happen if a curveball was thrown your way? If the path was to suddenly split before your very eyes, giving you an option you didn't think you had? If things didn't go to plan, so your confidence felt as burnt as that toast you forgot about this morning? (Or was that just me?)

What I've found, through example and experience, is that having a deep belief and a light attachment to our dreams is how we can continue to find the power to believe in ourselves and work towards our goals. Then if things don't go to (your) plan, you're still okay. You haven't pinned everything on just one dream, and so your dreams live on.

Envisioning your future (visioning it, and feeling into it, and seeing yourself right where you want to be) is important and necessary, but so is trusting that things will pan out as they're supposed to, for your highest good, even if that absolutely sucks in the moment.

You know that old saying about a journey of a thousand miles beginning with a single step?

Embodying deep belief and light attachment is about enjoying the journey—loving the process of building your biz, of writing your book, of creating the fabric pattern, of painting your art, of evolving your career, whatever it is—so that all your hopes and dreams don't depend on the outcome.

You can be happy now; you can be proud now; you can be successful now.

One more thing ... sometimes commanding yourself to be less attached creates even more attachment. So make sure to ask yourself gently.

Control is an illusion

Whenever I have let go of an outcome, I've allowed myself to flow and receive more than I ever could have, had I stayed in the place of attachment. It can feel counterintuitive—to let go, in order to receive. Doubt can seep in: *But if I let go, how can I call it in? That makes no sense.* And so it's in that space, the space that has you questioning your own power, where you must fill yourself up with trust and belief, letting go of the notion that this is only up to you.

Remember that while you can't control everything, you can always stay in your power with what you're creating and calling in.

You have to let go of what Control says: 'I want things to turn out exactly like this ... I'll decide how things should go.' Instead, you have to lean into what Power says: 'I'll show up as best I can. Whatever happens, I have the power to be okay, from within.'

Trying to control your dreams, or an outcome, or the details you don't know yet, can make you leak and leach and lose your power.

On the flip side, when you realise you always have the power to uplift your thoughts, to not buy into your inner critic's chatter, to align your energy, and to stay directed towards your bigger picture, you give power to your most powerful self. When you stay in your power, you can make the changes (and say the words, and do the things) that make all the difference.

Control is an illusion; your power is what matters. By uncovering and taking this on board, I have allowed myself to fill the space of attachment with one of deep belief that 'I've got this' but also that, if I don't, I'll still be okay; I'll course-correct and learn from the experience.

Something doesn't have to go wrong for you to learn from it; your trust can teach you things too.

Having a deep belief doesn't mean you're trying to set your future in stone. You can't anyway—it's fluid and ever-changing, because we have free will and there is always synchronicity at play. Acknowledging this helps you show up with more soul and less entitlement (that sense that you 'should' receive what you expect, because you worked so hard for it).

Of course you worked for it. Of course you put love and devotion on the line. Of course you showed up. But that doesn't mean you 'deserve' things to go your way.

Entitlement is a pre-emptive request for what we desire. It demands that we receive 'just because'. It tricks our ego into thinking that success is linked to our external achievements and nothing else. It unconsciously places huge pressure on ourselves to achieve perfection, when perfection is unattainable. It's the opposite of showing up with soul and saying, 'I'm here and I'm doing the work. It might work, and it might not. But still, here I stand.'

It's a collaborative effort

Becoming aligned and unstoppable while you work towards your dreams, actualise your goals and ground yourself in the new vision of what you're creating takes a collaborative effort. You are co-creating this vision with the Universe and a deeper, higher power, but you are also always choosing yourself.

You are blending fate and free will. You know that while this isn't only up to you, you have to take action to turn the milk of your dreams into the butter of your future.

When you allow yourself to enjoy this process and release the outcome; when you have a deep belief in yourself and in what you're creating; and when you have a light attachment of how it'll be perceived outside of yourself, only then can you keep showing up, keep creating, keep making, and keep believing in yourself and what you're co-creating and calling in.

JOURNALLING PROMPTS

— Where do you feel you need to let go of control?
— Where can you now lean into your power (and trust)?

ALIGNED AND UNSTOPPABLE AFFIRMATION

I believe in myself and what I'm co-creating and calling in. I trust in my own power, in my own free will, and in how my dreams are being supported by something greater than myself.

CHAPTER 5

It's Who You Already Are

Here's something you might not fully believe (yet), but that I hope to change your mind on (soon). You don't have to be perfect, to be successful and visible.

In fact, I believe it's quite the opposite. I believe that to be successful (you'll define that for yourself in just a moment) and visible, you have to be willing to be seen in your imperfect light; to show yourself for who you are; and to be yourself, knowing that you can't control the outcome.

This doesn't mean you need to overshare, find yourself feeling vulnerable in your sharing (in a way that leaves you itching to hide away), or make it all about sharing your life and not about teaching, supporting or empowering others along the way.

Rather, it means you allow yourself to be seen, and trust that by letting others see you, you allow yourself to see them too. And when we see others—when we really see others—that is when we can lift them up alongside ourselves, that is when we can support them, and that is when we can move, grow, evolve and connect alongside them.

In real time as I write this chapter, I recently held two client sessions in the same day where this idea of being 'imperfect, successful and visible' came up. Both of these wonderful clients are working towards deepening their own work, message and impact in their start-up businesses. And they're worried about it.

They're worried that being imperfect means clients won't want to work with them. They're worried that being imperfect means they're not allowed to be visible. And underneath it all, they wonder how they'll ever impact on the people they most want to support, with the energy they most wish to extend, if they continue to believe that they can't be successful or visible if they're not perfect.

One of my clients, Amber, is a coach. (FYI, all client names have been changed.) I asked her how she'd feel if she were to ever work with a coach who she deemed was 'perfect'—one who'd never experienced the issues or problems she had; one who'd never experienced difficult times; one who'd never had worries, doubts or fears. In other words, someone who couldn't really relate to her experiences at all. Of course, Amber's answer was that she wouldn't feel all that great about it. So I asked her why she felt she needed to be perfect, in order to attract the women she most wants to work with.

If feeling others' pain, if knowing their fears and understanding what they're feeling and experiencing is how we can truly connect with others, then isn't that the (most perfect) way forwards?

If I'd never experienced fears or blocks, worries or doubts, failure or a lack of momentum in relation to my business, my writing, my creativity and my dreams, how on earth could I have written this book? And, why on earth would you even want to read it?

In a nutshell, it would have been very short and go something like this:

I left high school and I knew exactly what I wanted to do. I started my business with no fears or hesitations, and everything went absolutely perfectly from the start. I was fully booked within just a few minutes! I had the most perfect website straight off the bat. I never had a tech issue; I never experienced self-doubt; I never felt overwhelmed; I always knew I was doing enough; and I never ever worried about how to pay the bills (or myself).

I had no boundary issues to work through; I never burnt myself out; and because I always had extremely high self-confidence, I never had to deepen my confidence within myself, because obviously I'm perfect. Every workshop I ever ran sold out within seconds. I received hundreds of thousands of emails every month from people asking to work with me, but obviously no way, as I did not have availability! Oh, and 271 publishing houses got in touch before I'd even started my Instagram account, because they just knew I had a New York Times bestselling book inside me. And then, you know, Oprah called! But obviously, she was going to call. Gosh, life and biz is just so good when you're perfect!

Ha! As if. Also ... vomit.

Essentially, it would have read like a completely made-up (and quite cringe-inducing, boring and narcissistic) fairytale, but without the necessary moment (or many moments) when the hero/heroine of the story actually faces their vulnerability and fears, then does what they're most called to do anyway.

It wouldn't be real, and you wouldn't want to read it, because it would be so far from your truth, from your story, and from your experiences. There's beauty in trying, in taking imperfect action, in trusting that you're exactly where you're supposed to be.

Underneath it all, this fear that we can't be seen or successful if we're not perfect is a perception we must shift. And underneath that is a desire to be accepted and acknowledged, witnessed and seen.

To have others do so, we must first do so within. So, accept, acknowledge, witness and see yourself. Validate yourself. Trust in your innate worth, in your enoughness, and in the enoughness of your work.

Instead of trying to carve out a 'perfect' version of yourself in what you're working towards, just be yourself. It's all you have to be. And the best part is that it's who you are already.

JOURNALLING PROMPTS

— What are you most scared to reveal to others?

— Why are you scared to be vulnerable or seen in this way?

— Can you think of anyone—perhaps someone you admire—who's shared their own vulnerabilities? If so, how did seeing that make you feel?

— What could being your true self and taking imperfect action inspire others to do/think/feel?

— If you let yourself be yourself, what's the best that could happen?

— If you let yourself be yourself, what's the worst that could happen? (And would that really be so bad?)

ALIGNED AND UNSTOPPABLE AFFIRMATION

I see myself for all that I am, and I let this shine out into the world. It's safe for me to be seen and to be visible. I honour, validate, accept and respect myself, knowing this supports others to do the same.

CHAPTER 6

You Can Change Your Mind(set)

It was a Sunday night and it felt like I was at rock bottom. I was seriously thinking about quitting my business and finding a job. But what that job might be, I had no idea.

Feeling utterly panicked, overwhelmed and confused, I turned to my hubby, tears streaming down my cheeks. Nic asked me, 'What would be the most amazing that could happen right now?'

'If someone purchased my top 1:1 coaching package, that would be amazing. That would be the absolute best thing that could happen right now.' I half-smiled as I said it, because it felt so impossible and far away. *Who would be browsing my coaching packages late on a Sunday night?* I thought to myself with disdain.

I followed Nic to the kitchen to chat while he made dinner (yeah, he's the chef in our house; I'm a lucky lady). I poured myself a huge glass of red wine and sat down in a slump, taking big gulps though my tears.

I took a deep, shaky breath and decided to let it all go—the fear, the worry, the concern—and just focus on what I could control, align and balance: my energy, thoughts and actions. I decided to stop thinking of myself as a victim in this situation, enjoy the rest of the evening, and look at everything with fresh eyes in the morning.

Just before dinner was ready, I went back to where my phone lay on the couch and picked it up. On the home screen sat a PayPal notification, for the exact amount of the program I'd just mentioned to Nic. A new client had indeed signed up to my top coaching package.

Like a Disney cartoon character, my jaw actually dropped. I thought I needed a moment to sit down on the couch, but as soon as I did so, excitement and relief took over. I leapt back up again to race into the kitchen, brandishing my phone in hubby's face with the biggest, silliest grin on mine.

Nic looked at me as if to say, 'Of course!' I'd received the most incredible confirmation from my business, the Universe and the energy of my own desires; I was still on track, still able to receive, still in the right place, and still able to ask for something, shift my mindset, get out of my own way, and receive (without needing to constantly hustle either).

I'd let myself fall and feel it all, and then I'd given myself a very clear choice: stay where I was and continue to feel like a victim, or drink the wine and find a new way forward tomorrow. I chose the latter (and not just because it included wine).

The gift of choice

When I'm working with my business alignment clients, I have a saying they all know well: *It's your business, and your choice.*

It sounds so simple, but when we give ourselves the gift of choice—in whatever we're working towards, and however we're working towards it—we free up so many possibilities and draw them closer to us.

This means you can change ...

— **Your mindset:** 'I don't know how to do this' can shift to 'I'm learning something new every day, and I'll get to where I need to be, all in good time.'

— **Your thoughts:** 'No-one will ever want what I'm offering' can shift to 'I'm creating something valuable and needed; it brings me joy and supports those I'm most here to serve, and that is perfect.'

— **Your energy:** Depletion and lack of motivation can morph into alignment and flow.

— **Your actions:** Taking action from a place of fear or lack can shift into taking purposeful, aligned action that reinforces your commitment to yourself, your vision and your dreams.

— **Your strategy:** Hustling to burnout can cease to be your strategy; instead, you inject soul into your game plan, so that your actions become supercharged and way more impactful.

— **Your goals:** Instead of putting pressure on yourself to reach specific goals, you open up to all levels of receivership available to you, trusting that you can get to where you want to be via multiple routes.

— **Your dreams:** Instead of following the dreams of a past version of yourself, you can let the old go and follow the path of the new (even if that feels stretchy and uncertain).

— **Your current way of doing something:** It's your business/project/passion ... and your choice. Really.

— **Your offerings and direction:** Instead of doing things the way you've always done them, give yourself permission to pivot and change your mind when it feels right and true for you.

— **Your attention and focus:** Feeling like you 'should' focus your attention somewhere ceases to be your driving force; you start to invest your energy where it really matters.

Our mindset is everything. When I've gone through hard times, the harder I thought they were, the harder they felt. My mindset was everything, meaning I could also shift out of struggle and into surrender. Don't get me wrong—I've held plenty of pity parties for myself. But I can honestly say they've never made an inch of difference in my moving in a positive direction.

When I've taken responsibility for how I was feeling and reconnected to my intuition, deeper purpose and inner power, then I've been able to turn the volume down on my inner critic, and call my inner ally back into the room (where she was desperately needed). This meant that I could start to allow myself to not take things personally, to let myself feel the struggle and transmute it into something that could create a stronger base for myself. Then I could see the beauty in what I was creating, and my work felt lighter and easier.

My struggles felt healthier; they weren't happening to punish me, or only happening to me. Knowing this supported me in moving through them, in letting them go, in using them as fuel to rocket myself forwards.

In this way, I could let myself move from A to B with less struggle and more flow; with less expectation and pressure; with more ease and grace—because I allowed my mindset to support me.

A supportive mindset is one that's based on compassion; one that allows you to be adaptable and quick-thinking; one that helps you feel supported and on track, as you move towards your goals.

When you make the shift to support yourself—when you let yourself change your mind—you'll see the effects of making positive changes in your life and business, as well as the effects and impact this shift can make on your mood, energy system and vibration.

There'll be a moment of change for you too. Okay, let's be honest, there'll be many moments. There'll be many moments where you're called to reassert yourself in the workplace, in your business, in your career, and in your life. It's when this moment arises that you'll turn to face your doubts and say fiercely, 'You think that'll sway me? I'll show you what I've got. I'm just getting started.'

You can change your mind, and you can change your thoughts. You can stop feeling like a victim; you can stop thinking that you're not doing enough; you can stop thinking you're sabotaging yourself in ways you don't understand.

I believe that sometimes we think we're secretly self-sabotaging if things aren't going to 'our plan', yet we can't work out why. We take it too personally and think it's because we haven't done enough. Aah! This is when we're called to surrender, trust, show up and let go. It's not always (or only) up to us. There'll always be trust to lean into; a bigger plan at play; and the timing of new beginnings that asks us to be patient, while the details are worked out just out of sight.

You won't fall off the earth

Before we knew the earth was round, sailors used to fear they'd travel too far and fall off the side of the earth. You can imagine a sailor from that period feeling a little nervous when travelling far and wide. If you believed that going the distance meant certain death from freefalling into a black hole of nothingness, of course you'd be scared of sailing far away.

But we are not sailors (or maybe you are, but at least you now know that the earth is round!) and we don't have to fear freefalling into a black hole of nothingness by going the distance.

In fact, it's when we allow ourselves to trust that we're in this for the long run that we can really go the distance, take the pressure off ourselves, continue to show up for ourselves and our dreams, and put in the work that really matters.

This is when small wins become momentous, when momentum creates more opportunities, and when little dips, failures and plateaus cease to grind us to a halt. Because you know—you really know!—that you can go the distance; that you're in this for the right reasons; that you won't give up on yourself; and that you're here for the long haul.

Become aware to clear your fears

I have a memory of being really small and swimming in a dark-tiled pool. The effect of sunshine on the dark tiles meant that the water looked a murky dark blue-black. Whoever I was playing with decided it'd be a good idea to play 'sharks'. (Not to spoil the ending, but that is never a good idea when swimming in a pool that looks as deep and dark as the ocean.)

At one stage, my mind took this game to the next level, and not in a fun Mario Kart way. It stopped feeling like a pretend game, and started to feel all too real for me. I told myself there was a shark below me, and so I started panicking, seeing things in the water that were definitely not there.

To put this a tastier way: when you open a packet of salt and vinegar chips, does your mouth water? Hmm, salt and vinegar chips. (Ah, my mouth just watered as I wrote that! Our brains are so smart.) I'm guessing you said 'yes'. So if your mouth waters when you see or smell (or even think about) salt and vinegar chips, what happens to your body and energy when you make up stories about yourself, or when you tell yourself negative things, and then believe them?

It's the same when you create something, or work towards something. It's the same when you apply for a job, or open for business, or launch a new product or program. If you tell yourself there's danger and expectation everywhere, that's what you'll see, because it's what you believe.

If you tell yourself you'll fail, you'll think you're about to freefall into a black hole of nothingness. If you don't really look within, you'll start to see things that aren't there.

All those fears you're carrying ... are they really true?

Let's dig deep

Grab your journal or a notebook. At the top, scribble down your current goal (anything that you're working towards). Not sure what you're working towards? Write that down.

Now, write out how you're currently feeling about your goal (or goals, or lack thereof). What's your mindset around this? Write down all the fears you're carrying around in relation to that goal coming to fruition, and the fears around it not coming to fruition.

Look at it from every angle, every perspective. Don't fear writing down your negative thoughts, fears or beliefs around this; you have to be aware of these blocks in order to clear them.

As you write these negative thoughts and fears down, become aware of any stories, memories or 'rules' around them. Perhaps they are other people's beliefs you've taken on as your own; old memories that have become the story of today; old ways of doing things that you know aren't serving you anymore.

Now, it's time to clear away these negative thoughts and fears:

— You can do this through forgiveness work (it can be as simple as placing one hand on your journal page and one hand on your heart, sending yourself/someone else love and forgiveness).

— You can use the Emotional Freedom Technique, also known as EFT. We'll go through this in more detail soon; but if you don't want to wait, simply search for 'Emotional Freedom Technique' or 'EFT tapping' online to find the script and the acupressure points to tap.

— You can continue to journal about these beliefs, allowing guidance to come through by learning more and more about yourself, so that you can deeply know how to move on.

— You can see a kinesiologist to help you clear the blocks, and/or a reiki healer or therapist.

— You can practise yoga, do some daily meditation, and cultivate a deeper connection to yourself through stillness and by listening to yourself, to help you know what you need most.

You can try any or all of the above to see what works for you—in your own way, in your own time, and with compassion and gentleness.

Unlimiting beliefs

We so often talk about limiting beliefs, right? Part of what you just did was to become aware of them. So now, let's create some unlimiting beliefs.

In my book, *It's All Good*, I wrote:

Will you be ready to let go of your old limits, expand, integrate and uplevel? Will you let the energy you stand in, the ground you stand on, become more expansive, hold you more steadily, and feel illimitable? Of course you will. Of course you can. That's why you're here.

What could you expand into now? What could some of your unlimiting beliefs be? Here are some ideas:
— Instead of thinking *It's going to be such hard work to do what I love,* think to yourself *I'm ready to work for what I want, and allow in joy and ease while I do so.*
— Instead of thinking *I don't have what it takes,* think to yourself *I'm ready to do this, and to work towards my dreams and goals.*
— Instead of thinking *Who am I to do this?* think to yourself *I'm worthy of receiving my dreams and goals, or something better.*
— Replace the limiting belief of *It's always such a struggle,* with *It's safe for me to receive.*
— Swap *I can't succeed in case I upset someone,* for *It's safe for me to be seen succeeding.*
— Instead of thinking *I don't know what to do next,* think *It's safe for me to trust myself.*
— Instead of wondering *I don't know if I'm capable,* think *I am confident, aligned and unstoppable.*

Take some time to write down your own unlimiting beliefs now. They're most likely the direct opposite of your fears. Start listening to these beliefs, and acting from this place.

Your future self
Another great way to start to clear away limiting beliefs, reprogram your mind and expand your energy is to start connecting with your future self, and to what you wish to see, feel, have, experience, do, and embody in the future. Grab your journal or a notebook, and

write out a script 'as if' you were already experiencing everything you wish to experience, already embodying everything you're working towards, and already feeling/doing/having/being all that you wish to feel/do/have/be.

This isn't about future tripping or feeling like you're not 'there yet'; it's about creating an internal pathway to your future, building a bridge between 'then' and 'now', and rewiring your brain and neural pathways so you can truly visualise and make space for your ideal future.

You may like to use some of the unlimiting beliefs you just created, when you do this exercise.

Let it be a slow burn

To create and receive your dreams and goals, you have to keep 'going in'—going into the places that help you create; the places that scare you; the places that push you, expand you, rock you, ground you.

You have to keep going the distance, to get to where you want to be. You have to keep envisioning yourself there, and believe it's possible.

We're so used to quick Instagram posts and videos, flashes of likes, shares and comments, all equating to quick dopamine bursts from social media. But writing a book, building your body of work, your business, career or empire ... that's going to take as much time as it needs, and that's perfect.

Let it be a slow burn, so that you don't use all your fuel at the beginning. Let things take time to grow. Trust the process of not rushing. Start thinking like the sailor who knows the world is round. Start by trusting that you're supported, and that you can go the distance.

Start believing in yourself, your future, and your unlimiting beliefs—the ones that support you to step up, show up, step out and do the work you know you're here to do.

Remember that you have an innate power to change your thoughts and adapt to a more positive way of seeing yourself and your world, knowing that your thoughts affect your actions, energy and ability to receive.

This doesn't mean you can't look at your fears, for fear they'll manifest. It means you must look at them, become aware of them, clear them away in whatever way serves you best, then take action from that space.

Start by knowing, deep down, that you are held and supported (because you are).

ALIGNED AND UNSTOPPABLE AFFIRMATION

I trust in my innate power to uplift my thoughts, supporting my energy, actions and ability to receive, as I work towards what matters most to me. I believe in what I'm calling in next.

CHAPTER 7

Go Through It First

'Everyone who studies natural medicine is here to heal themselves first.' That's what my lecturer told us on our first day in naturopathy college, and I could totally get it.

Long before I started studying natural medicine, I'd been interested in herbal medicine and food as medicine. I was also finally starting to feel myself coming out of a few years of poor body image and the ups and downs of dieting. Of course, I wanted to help other people, but I also wanted to help and heal myself.

Years later, having witnessed huge pivots in my business, passion and body of work, I still believe that we teach what we most want to deepen within ourselves. And on some level, no matter what you're creating, no matter what you're working on sharing, this is true for you too.

As you begin to deepen your confidence in using your voice, you need to understand and accept this, so you can use it as a tool to expand, and possibly even share and teach your work.

The more you accept it, the more you will feel connected to your bigger picture, and the more real, vulnerable and approachable you will be to your clients, customers, colleagues, readers, audience and tribe—whoever needs to be in your orbit.

And this is how you'll build and expand the energy of your creations, business, career and body of work.

Your clients are less likely to support you if you're a cookie-cutter wellness guru; or a personal trainer who seems perfect; or a business owner (or human in general) who always has everything altogether. If you're a health coach and all you do is talk about green smoothies, chia seed pudding and kale, your clients won't feel connected to you on a deeper level. So at the end of the day, you're the one who'll miss out on both cultivating deeper relationships with others and supporting your clients in the best way possible.

Of course, you can talk about all of those things if you want, but be real about it! Talk about the smoothie you made for breakfast, but also about how you then dropped it all over the kitchen counter as you ran out the door late for an appointment. Talk about the lessons you've learnt and how we might learn them too. Tell us what's not working for you, and what you're going to do about it.

Trying to show up as being perfect is a recipe for dissatisfaction, because you can never achieve perfection. And you won't resonate with your most loving and ideal community, if they think you're so far removed from their reality. Your community want to know the real you.

However, that doesn't mean you have to overshare or tell us your home address. It doesn't mean you have to share in a way that makes you feel uncomfortably vulnerable. It doesn't mean you have to share while you're in the midst of your pain. Instead, it asks you to share the parts of you that are going to touch the hearts, minds and souls of the people you're here to serve most, when you're ready to, and in a way that feels good to you.

(On that note, I prefer to process how I'm feeling, before opting to share it publicly. In this way, I am less emotionally charged and can rationally decide what is helpful to share, and what needs to stay within the private pages of my journal, the private hallways and chambers of my mind and heart, or in private conversations with family, friends and healers.)

Your community, audience and tribe (whatever word you want to use) want to know that you've felt what they've felt, that you've seen what they're going through, and that you've shared their struggles, frustrations, pain and overwhelm.

How do I know this? Because back when I started my business, I used to worry that I wouldn't be taken seriously as a nutritionist, because I thought I wasn't skinny enough. I thought I would be judged, ridiculed and laughed at, because it looked like I hadn't 'got my sh*t together'. I was nervous that if a client came to me for weight loss advice, they wouldn't trust me.

How silly (but totally understandable) of me. My clients loved me more because I had felt their pain; they could feel that, when we spoke about their pain. They could feel it when I offered up gentle suggestions, and when I shared stories of my own to help them on their path forward. It helped them feel understood. Most importantly, they didn't feel alone in their pain and struggle to find body positivity.

The same goes for clients who came to me with anxiety, depression or fatigue. I have felt all of those things in my life, which made all the difference in how the prescriptions and suggestions I offered my clients supported them.

And now the same goes for my clients who are feeling overwhelmed in their businesses, lives or creative endeavours; who are wanting to align their energy and call in what's next; who are wanting to connect with themselves on a deeper level; and who are wanting to clear away perfectionism, procrastination and comparison and anything else that might be holding them back from loving what they create in their businesses and lives.

I'm not saying you always have to have gone through what your clients are going through—that's not true all the time. And you are not always your own ideal client, and that's more than okay.

But it's highly likely you'll end up attracting a community, clients and an audience (also friends!) who are going through what you've been through in your life—something you've already deepened within yourself, or something you're still (and always) deepening.

Think of how a beautiful pearl is created: an irritant enters an oyster; to protect itself, the oyster secretes mother-of-pearl, coating the irritant in this protective mineral substance, which eventually forms the beautiful pearl.

Just as an irritant creates beauty in an oyster, your pain can create your purpose.

Live your message

Months before my first book, *You Are Enough*, was published, I read an article by a well-known author who said that when you write and publish non-fiction, you'll be called to live your message. I remember thinking to myself: *Hmm, that sounds interesting. I wonder if that'll play out for me too.*

And then ... right about the time my book was published, my skin broke out with the most horrible adult acne I'd ever experienced. This was the absolute worst time for a severe breakout. I had to call on my self-confidence and know my worth, even though my skin made me feel incredibly self-conscious. I had to remember that I was enough. I had to live my message; I had to keep showing up, anyway.

Fast forward to the months leading up to the publication of *It's All Good*, and I was called to live my message again. Much of what I'd written about came up again in my life: lessons I had already lived through; fears I'd already looked at; thoughts I'd already cleared away. I had to let go, trust and surrender. I had to live my message; I had to keep showing up anyway.

It's happened again with this book. Throughout the writing process, I've had to deepen every single thing I've written about. I've had to live my message over and over again, in order to keep writing this book, in order to finish this book. I've had to keep showing up anyway.

Since I've become aware of this, I find it often happens. If I'm about to launch something, speak about something, teach something or write about something, I'll be reminded of it. It's not always a painful reminder—it can be joyful too. But it'll be a reminder in some way, shape or form of how far I've come; of what I still need to deepen within myself; of what I must remember in order to teach this work better; of what I can still release, clear, heal, activate, embody and transform within myself.

So if you find yourself going through something now, let yourself go through it, knowing you can use the experience as fuel for later. Know you can absorb these lessons and transform them into teachings. Know this could become fodder for your next project, meeting, book, artwork, course, program, or just your next girls' dinner.

Let yourself go through it first; let it deepen within you, so that you can share it with the world. After all, how can we reach for the stars, if we aren't grounded in our truth?

If it comes back again and again (as it may), let the old lessons wash over you, let yourself see it with new eyes, a new perspective. Let yourself learn it all over again, knowing it's for your highest good ... and that it'll make a great tale around ~~the campfire~~ Instagram.

It can feel difficult to go through lessons sometimes, especially when we find ourselves having to relearn lessons we think we've already learnt. However it's always worth it, if you can use this knowledge to deepen what you're learning and teaching yourself, and by extension of this, what you may wish to share with others.

By deepening what you most need to learn, you can then teach it in the best way. And that's how you can create, call your power back to you, and find stable and secure ground on which to build your dreams and activate your self-trust.

JOURNALLING PROMPTS

— What are you currently deepening within yourself?
— Are you relearning any old lessons? What could they be teaching you in a new light now?
— What are you going through now that may be able to help someone else later?

ALIGNED AND UNSTOPPABLE AFFIRMATION

I'm aligned to deepening my inner wisdom and knowledge, so I can best share this with the world.

CHAPTER 8

Success as Defined by You

Success is liking yourself,
liking what you do, and liking how you do it.

MAYA ANGELOU

To feel successful in your endeavours, you must know what this really means to you.

What does success mean to you? You might have been asked this question before, and to be honest, it's not always easy to answer. We're constantly bombarded by ideas of what external success should look like, and it usually looks very glossy. But rarely does it tell the whole story, as external success doesn't always mean internal fulfilment.

In his book *Herding Tigers*, Todd Henry writes: *Many people lack a clear definition of success in their own mind, so they spend their entire career chasing vapor.*

If you only define your success by what you want other people to see (like your social media stats), or by what you tell other people, or by the amount of money in your bank account, or how many clients you have, then you may never feel the sense of internal joy and satisfaction that can come through doing work that lights you up.

If you hold your self-worth at arm's length, scrutinising it under the harsh light of external success, you give other people and external situations (that might be completely out of your control) too many opportunities to snatch it away from you.

Don't let your measure of success be based on comparison. Let it come from within; let it be your own.

Hold your self-worth in the vessel of yourself. Keep it safe, nurture it, see it in the best light, let it hold and support you, let it tell you what success means to you.

The truth is that who you are is more important than where you are or what you're doing. You could be the most 'successful' person and treat others poorly, or be incredibly unhappy, or never feel like you've done enough. Or you could define success on your own terms, stay in alignment with yourself and your values, and light the way for others because of it.

Does success mean you wake up and find joy in your work? Does it mean, as the inimitable late Maya Angelou said: *Success is liking yourself, liking what you do, and liking how you do it?*

To like yourself, you must stay in integrity. You must show up in a way that best serves and supports you, in order to best serve and support others.

To like what you do, you must make space to create, back yourself and your work, and allow yourself to love what you create.

To like how you do it, you must create pockets of joy that fuel your work and fire up your dreams.

I find it's easier to define and enjoy success if I know what I'm working towards in my own life and business; if I've set goals that feel deeply aligned to the greater vision I hold for my life (even if those goals feel big and far away).

Ask yourself these questions:

— What are you working towards now?
— How do you want to feel as you move towards it?
— How do you want to feel when you know it's been achieved/ not achieved?
— How can you continue to anchor into your deeper purpose and meaning, whether you achieve this goal or not?

Your answers will guide and sculpt your definition of what success feels like to you, and help you stop drooling over glossy pictures on Instagram that tell you one side of one story of one person's moment from one day. (It's just a tiny snapshot of real life. You know that, yet sometimes you let it affect your day, your energy, your actions, and even your potential, right?)

Celebrate your success

I think it's so important to celebrate your successes. How can we call in more of what we desire, if we can't celebrate and be grateful for what we've already received? We need to stop and smell the roses we planted years ago, before thinking about the ones blooming ahead on our path.

Here are some ideas to help you celebrate your successes ...

Tell someone about it

Share your success, shamelessly, without guilt, staying small, or playing it down. Don't pretend it was luck that got you here. Luck might play a tiny part, but to underplay yourself is to undermine yourself; and that's the opposite of being in alignment with your highest self, with being aligned to your dreams, and with being unstoppable in your deep drive and devotion to creating what calls to you.

Anchor into it

Feel it and hold it within, so that you can continue to draw more of it towards you. Do this through intention, mindset, breath and gratitude. Do it by being present in the moment; this is where you are, this is what you've called in, this is what you've created. Ground into that.

Thank the Universe and ask for more

Do this by simply saying 'thank you', and by envisioning and embracing the truth that 'there's more where that came from'. You're allowed to be grateful and ask for more. You're allowed to trust that good things will keep flowing to you.

I used to think that if something went well, something bad would have to happen to even the scales. It was an old belief—a very limiting one at that—that meant I'd quickly and quietly sabotage myself, by not believing in myself if something had recently gone well for me.

(A brilliant example of this is when I received an unexpected tax refund of $900. About to go on holiday, I did a happy dance! Just hours later, I reversed my car into a pole in a parking garage. Because I didn't want to put it through my insurance and risk increasing my premium, I took it to a nearby garage to get fixed. The quote? Spot on $900.)

This type of sabotaging behaviour makes absolutely no sense. Imagine if horses thought like that while showjumping; they'd jump over the first jump effortlessly, then crash into the second;

they'd collect themselves and then fly over the third, baulking at the fourth. They'd go around the ring, fluctuating from *This is amazing; I have full faith in myself and my abilities!* to *Farrrrr out, I suck, what is happening? I have no idea who I am or what I'm working towards!* back to *I love what I do! I do what I love!*

I want to laugh, but I also want to cry, because that's what so many of us do. We spend our lives fluctuating from acceptance and belief to ambiguity and confusion. We do well, so we punish ourselves by thinking that it was a fluke, or luck, and we didn't really deserve it, so we ensure it doesn't happen again soon. But then, after a while we pull ourselves together and decide to get back in the game. Then we create and receive something wonderful, and the cycle starts again.

If that's you, I invite you to write out all your fears and perceived negative consequences of asking the Universe for more of what you already have. You'll know how to do this by simply thinking about receiving more, and noticing the thoughts, fears, beliefs or mental patterns around this.

For example, if you do speaking gigs and you think to yourself: *I'd love to put myself out there and do more corporate speaking engagements,* notice what you think of next.

That might lead you to think to yourself: *But if that happens, I'll become burnt out and exhausted. It will be such hard work to even find those opportunities and I'll probably land gigs I don't want to do, and then I won't be able to say 'no'. People will think I'm greedy for charging higher rates and getting lots of work. I'll start to resent receiving more opportunities, because it'll take me away from my other passions.*

Of course, you might only notice a couple of negative thoughts, or you might write out pages of them. Whatever comes up and through for you is perfect, so honour it and don't judge yourself for these thoughts. You're bringing them to the surface, so your awareness and actions can help clear them away.

You might find some of the points you write down sound ridiculous to your conscious mind. That's totally normal, and actually shows that you've tuned into a deeper layer of your fears. So don't be ashamed of what comes through when you do this exercise; just write everything down (even if you cringe/cry/laugh at yourself for doing so).

Then forgive yourself for being so hard on yourself. Place your hands on your heart and say, 'I'm so sorry you think that receiving more is going to be hard work. I'm so sorry that you think people will judge you for doing well. I'm so sorry you thought you didn't deserve more of the good things you already have in your life. I forgive you, I love you.'

Then do some inner work to clear away those fears. Sit with the thoughts you've put on paper, and send love and gratitude to them for trying to keep you safe. I suggest doing some Emotional Freedom Technique tapping to clear the stress around it. (If you're not familiar with tapping, keep reading for a suggested script.) Use this new awareness to help you shift the old thought patterns, with gentleness and compassion.

Emotional Freedom Technique (EFT)

EFT is a simple and powerful tool that you can use to clear negative thought patterns and shift your energy, using the body's energy meridian points and neuro-linguistic programming.

Essentially, you tap on specific acupressure points on the body, while saying a specific script, and adding in a stress, fear or block to clear. For example: *Even though I [insert fear/limiting belief here], I deeply and completely love and accept myself.*

While there are slight variations on the acupressure points to tap (while saying the script to follow) the general points to tap are:
— Midline of head (imagine your hair is parted down the middle; tap gently on that line on your crown)
— Above your eyebrows
— On your temples
— Under your eyes
— Above your lip
— On your chin
— Just below your collarbones
— Just under your armpits (if you're wearing a bra, think bra strap area on either side of your torso)
— Pinky-finger side of each hand (doing one hand at a time)

This gives us nine points to tap, but we'll say ten clearing statements, as we'll use the opportunity to tap on the side of each hand. Lightly tap on these points using your pointer and middle finger, using either one hand or both, while saying the script and adding in whatever it is you want to clear.

Here's a suggested script for an EFT balance (using common fears that often come up in sessions with my clients, when working towards big life, work and business goals):
— While tapping on the crown of your head: *Even though I don't know what the next step is, I deeply and completely love and accept myself.*
— While tapping above your eyebrows: *Even though I'm worried about making the wrong decision, I deeply and completely love and accept myself.*

— While tapping on your temples: *Even though I don't think anyone will like what I'm doing, I deeply and completely love and accept myself.*

— While tapping under your eyes: *Even though I'm nervous about what people I know will say or think, I deeply and completely love and accept myself.*

— While tapping above your lip: *Even though I don't know if I'll be able to make enough money from this, I deeply and completely love and accept myself.*

— While tapping on your chin: *Even though I feel so uncertain about the future, I deeply and completely love and accept myself.*

— While tapping just below your collarbones: *Even though I don't know if I'm good enough, I deeply and completely love and accept myself.*

— While tapping just under your armpits: *Even though I constantly compare myself to others and question my worth, I deeply and completely love and accept myself.*

— While tapping the pinky-finger side of your left hand: *Even though I don't think anyone will want to listen to what I have to say, I deeply and completely love and accept myself.*

— While tapping the pinky-finger side of your right hand: *Even though I feel so nervous about being seen and being visible, I deeply and completely love and accept myself.*

Now take a deep breath in and out.

You can run yourself through the suggested fears/blocks I've just listed; then next time you do this, instead of saying the suggested fears/blocks I've included, add in your own.

When to use EFT

You can use EFT whenever you want, to support your physical, mental, emotional and spiritual health. You can do as many rounds as you like, whenever you need to.

I was first taught how to do EFT when seeing a holistic counsellor many years ago. It helped me to calm the anxiety I'd been feeling, start trusting myself more, and feel confident enough to leave a relationship that wasn't making me happy.

At first, I used it for mental/emotional support only. Years later, on the day of my very first corporate speaking engagement, I found myself suffering from the worst period pain of my life. I'd taken every herb possible, as well as paracetamol and ibuprofen, used heat packs and the like, yet nothing was working. I was becoming increasingly stressed out (which was also not helping). I decided to do some EFT, using the script: *Even though I have the worst period pain of my entire life and I don't know how I'll do my talk tonight, I deeply and completely love and accept myself.*

I repeated the same words for every tapping point, and did three full rounds of the points. As soon as I finished that third round, my pain disappeared. Disappeared. I blinked, took a deep breath, got up from my fetal position lying on my office floor, got dressed and ran a successful event.

I now use EFT on an almost daily basis to clear stresses and thoughts that feel like they're holding me back (even if it's something as seemingly insignificant as receiving an email that makes me want to grind my teeth). I especially use it when setting goals or intentions, noticing what limiting beliefs come up, knowing I can clear them away.

What to do after an EFT balance

Take a deep breath and drop it all; leave it in the past. Then come back to yourself and your centre.

Repeat as necessary.

ALIGNED AND UNSTOPPABLE AFFIRMATION

I create my own version of success, being grateful for all I've already created, and all that's still to come.

CHAPTER 9

Allow the Unfolding

Love only what falls your way and is fated for
you. What could suit you more than that?
MARCUS AURELIUS, *MEDITATIONS*

I was working with a client named Madison. For months, she
had been worried about where she was heading, and whether
she would be able to call in what was next for her. We had a
kinesiology alignment session and she told me she'd just written
in her journal: *When will it ever be enough? When will I ever be okay?*

Madison said she was ready to be supported in a bigger way;
to stand up and allow herself to receive without fear; to watch
the unfolding of all she'd been working so diligently towards.

So we got straight into it. We created some goals together, and
dived into a kinesiology balance. These were the goals to which
we aligned her:

— I am ready to be supported in a bigger way.
— I easily welcome in new amazing clients in supportive numbers.
— Everything is in place for me to earn more money easily.
— I am ready for the next step.
— I can slow down and still receive money and clients.

— I can easily and beautifully manage everything on my plate.
— My work and business are enough.
— I allow my business to grow.
— I'm on the right path with my life.
— I know and trust that I can do this.

The very first energy-balancing remedy that came up for her was the Bach flower essence Gorse, plus the Gate of Hope acupressure point, from the beautiful book, *Floral Acupuncture*.

According to Dr. Edward Bach, the Gorse essence is a remedy for those who've given up belief and lost faith in themselves and their situation. By using this essence, we can allow ourselves to trust there is a way forward. By doing so, we actually find and make our way ahead, looking towards the light.

The Gate of Hope is a point on the torso (just under your diaphragm, on the nipple line, on either side of your torso), which sits on the liver meridian. This acupressure point holds the energies of possibility, renewal and hope. Using the point helps to release stagnation and envision a positive future. In traditional Chinese medicine and kinesiology theory, the Gate of Hope point corresponds to the Wood element, which also relates to growth, new beginnings and renewal.

We went one step further, by using the essence on the acupressure point; this supports you to allow your hope to return, on an even deeper level. (Remember hope? That sweet, nurturing emotion that reminds you that you can dream in a positive way again.) This supports you in clearing away your own obstacles and opening your eyes to the bright possibilities that lie ahead.

If you wish, you can do something similar right now: simply use your pointer and middle finger on each hand to find the Gate of Hope point I described (it may feel a little tender). Hold the point with your fingers applying a firm but gentle pressure for 2-3 minutes, taking cleansing breaths in and out through your nose. You may feel a shift in energy, thoughts, mind and mood. Later on, you may want to purchase the Gorse flower essence to either put on the Gate of Hope point, or take orally.

As we continued our kinesiology balance, and as Madison started to tune back into flow and alignment, the message of the day was simple: she now had to allow this to unfold, without trying to control the outcome.

Allow an unfolding

We can feel very pressured by time, as we work towards our goals and our bigger vision. By putting undue pressure on ourselves, by listening to negative stories and limiting beliefs that simply aren't true, we can sometimes lose hope in the vision we're creating for ourselves. We can think that the growth and expansion we crave for is too far away.

As if conspiring in her favour, the cards that then fell out of the deck for Madison were 'Timing' and 'Patience'. This gentle reminder couldn't have been clearer: step back into flow, trust the timing, allow the unfolding of what you're working towards, of what you're envisioning, of what you're taking action on to draw towards you—and don't rush it.

This isn't about waiting impatiently. It's about grounding into what's next, making space, calling it in, and noticing how you feel when you embody what you're calling in (even before you've received it), all the while trusting in this space of new beginnings.

Push and mush mode

You know those times you feel so far away from how you want to feel, and from what you're calling in? This is when you need to become really aware of what story is holding you back, which fear is keeping you small, which negative thought or limiting belief is blocking your path.

In those times, you must tap into the energy of what you're hoping to expand into and receive, and switch it up; let your stress hold less tension and power over you, and let your expansion take hold.

Another one of my clients, Emma, had booked a session, in a panic. She'd been working so hard and had come into a real crisis of confidence. Seemingly out of nowhere, she felt completely irrelevant in her field, doubting everything she did, said, wrote or thought.

She was feeling anxious and small, tired and drained. She felt like she'd lost all connection to her intuition and guidance—to her system of higher and greater support. She told me she felt like a small boat rocking on the water, far out in the ocean. Every time she found a rope in the water, she'd pull on it, hoping it would lead her back to shore, but it wouldn't lead her anywhere, and a sense of panic would set in again.

She wasn't at the point of wanting to quit, just at the point of needing something to shift, to welcome in a sense of hope and trust, a rush of new energy and alignment.

'Sounds like you're in push and mush mode,' I said. I came up with this term one day while feeling sluggish, feeling like I was trying to push through, instead of just resting and restoring to step back into my flow. It's a term that explains that deep energetic drag and drain when you're in pushing mode, striving and working hard and actually getting nowhere, leaving you feeling drained and exhausted. AKA feeling like mush!

While we'll do another dive into self-care and doing your best work soon, let's make sure we're on the same page now. Pushing yourself to do your best work (often with the underlying thought that that's the only way to 'get ahead') is the opposite of being aligned and unstoppable, or clear and confident.

It's not a bad thing in and of itself. If you allow yourself to become aware of it and listen to it, it teaches you to slow down, reconnect, recommit, realign, and get back in the headspace and energy you need to be in, to do your best work, without rushing, forcing, striving or panicking.

'Let's just do a big clear-out, to bring you back to your centre and into alignment,' I suggested. So these are some of the kinesiology goals we went for:

— I know I am worthy.
— I am clear and confident.
— I am on the right path.
— I love what I do.
— It's safe for me to speak up in my business and life.
— I easily make the best decisions that benefit me and my business.
— I call my energy and my power back to me.
— I can easily and always call more money into my life and business.
— I trust myself, my intuition and my guidance.
— I am ready to call in what's next.

I then muscle tested Emma to find the key goal—the one that, out of every goal we'd created for her, was the most pertinent to her stepping back into full and true alignment:

— I can easily and always call more money into my life and business.

This core goal was, essentially, Emma's main block. The fear she was holding in her mind, body and energy field was holding her back from feeling calm, centred and committed to herself.

So I tested the percentage of stress and contraction, and of openness and expansion, in relation to this core goal. Lo and behold, she was at maximum stress (i.e. feeling very constricted, contracted, fearful and out of alignment) and minimum expansion (i.e. not feeling at ease, grounded, open, expansive, in flow or aligned).

These states were impacting on one another because to feel expansion, we must first let go of the belief that we are stuck. Her fear that she wouldn't be able to call more money into her life and work was causing such constriction that it was blocking her sense of ease, flow, alignment and abundance, as well as her belief in herself, impacting on almost every area of her life and business.

When we dived deeper into what this core goal meant for Emma, it became clear she'd taken comments from other people on board—people she loved and respected—that weren't for her absolute betterment. She said that lately she'd had plenty of conversations with friends in her industry who were saying how hard business was; how the market was saturated and things weren't like they used to be; how you had to change what you were doing in order to succeed 'these days'.

This had left her feeling as though she was completely powerless to change (and to make a change), to be of service, to make a difference, and to be supported by her life's work. She then said to me, 'Those conversations and the depleted energy I left them with, made me feel as though I'd lost touch with my own alchemy, trust and magic, by going so far down the rabbit hole of lack of faith and mistrust.'

We dug deeper. Emma loved and respected the people who'd given her their opinions so much, she was more invested in keeping their beliefs alive than in loving herself and her dreams. She realised that she had to let go of what those people had said, and honour herself and her own path now.

I asked her to work with her CEO self—the part of her that could rise above the current situation and vibration, the opinions and thoughts of others, and make her own beliefs matter. By doing so, I explained that she'd be able to 'flick the switch'—to start deeply believing in herself and her own ability to create what she wanted in her life and work, without feeling the need to take on others' opinions before (or instead of) her own.

Throughout the rest of our session, we worked to clear her sense of lack, to shift from 'push and mush mode' into alignment and trust, to allow the unfolding of what she was working towards, and to transmute her fears into a deep sense of harmony. We worked to ensure that she knew she could trust herself; that 'more' doesn't mean 'better'; that she had the power to shift her self-doubt, to change, and to transform.

And so do you.

AN ESSENCE FOR ALIGNMENT

Alongside Gorse, Cerato is another Bach flower essence that is very suited here. It supports you to have more faith and trust in your own judgement and decisions, allowing you to listen to your heart and intuition more, without feeling the need to take on the opinions of others.

You've got this

To support us in trusting and allowing an unfolding, instead of rushing and pushing ahead, we must also trust that by not controlling the unfolding, we're actually allowing it even more.

Lately I've been reading some of Marcus Aurelius' *Meditations*. Aurelius was a Roman emperor and philosopher. His *Meditations* are a series of his personal writings, thought to be dated around 161-180 AD when he was emperor, reflecting on spiritual and stoic philosophies.

I just pick up the book and flip it open, reading whatever page I land on. The latest paragraph I've landed on has left me feeling particularly calm and reconnected to life (after a rather intense couple of weeks, where I did plenty of 'zooming'—as my husband calls it—into the future): *Do not let the future trouble you. You will come to it (if that is what you must) possessed of the same reason that you apply now to the present.*

In today's talk, that's the equivalent of: 'Don't worry about the future so much. Stay in the present and trust that when you get to the 'future', you'll manage it with as much strength, grace and grit (or more!) as you do today.'

Said even more simply: you've got this.

The quote from Aurelius that opens this chapter is also particularly soothing. It's something to embody when you're zooming into the future, worrying, wondering and working yourself up into a lather, because pieces of your puzzle feel as though they don't quite fit today.

Trust that what is meant for you will not pass you by. Allow yourself to lean into, and allow, the unfolding of all that is to come.

ALIGNED AND UNSTOPPABLE AFFIRMATION

*I step into my flow, trust the timing, and allow
the unfolding of all I'm creating and receiving.*

Part 2

THE DEEPER WORK

Clearing Fears and Blocks

CHAPTER 10

Perfection Is Not Our Aim

I was six weeks pregnant, and feeling it. My mood was low, my mind was distracted, my brain was foggy and my body felt like it was filled with mud.

I was on my way into the city to give a corporate presentation to a roomful of marketing executives, to essentially pitch myself for a huge gig. I was so grateful for the opportunity, but my excitement was marred by brain fog and fatigue—part of me would've much rather been on the couch.

It was a cold, windy and rainy day. Roadworks in the city meant that the usual route needed a detour, and the closest my Uber driver could drop me was several hundred metres away from my destination. Also, I was wearing heels. Fab.

I hadn't felt as inspired or in flow as I usually did when I wrote and practised my presentation, and I certainly hadn't prepared in my usual way. Because of my brain fog, I hadn't felt like I could channel what I needed to while creating the presentation. I was worried that because I felt blocked, I wouldn't feel guided or supported by spirit/source during the presentation.

I felt like I was going in blind; underneath it all, I could feel butterflies flapping against my insides, flying up a storm. I wondered how I'd manage to speak about energy and alignment, and radiate and hold space in a corporate environment, when I wasn't feeling energised or aligned at all.

But ... I showed up, did the presentation as best I could, and landed the highest paying corporate engagement of my business to date.

All the while not being perfect.

You don't need to be perfect either

Alchemy, trust and magic are what alignment can feel like, when we're truly in it, trusting our path and allowing the unfolding that's to come. That's when things seem to just fall into our lap, appear out of the blue, drop in seamlessly and work out effortlessly.

It's what many of us strive for, and yet ... the way we work towards our dreams and goals can be complicated by pressure, tension, tightness and perfectionism. So I'd like to invite you to see things from the other side. Even if you don't feel magical and full of trust, this doesn't automatically mean you're not in alignment. If things don't effortlessly fall into your lap, that doesn't mean you've done something wrong, that things can't or won't go right for you, or that you're far away from your dreams.

Thinking that alignment means perfection is just another way we put pressure on ourselves to be perfect, and berate ourselves if things don't go to our exact plan. This is how I used to feel (and sometimes still need to remind myself about).

Good things can still flow to you, even if or when you're not feeling completely aligned. What might this look like in your everyday life?

— You might get a parking ticket, on the day a new client signs up to work with you.
— Your website might crash, just before an email arrives with an opportunity you never saw coming.
— Someone might say 'no' to you, and the next day the most incredible 'yes!' comes through unexpectedly.
— You might be feeling stressed out about money, telling yourself that the only way you'll make money is if you feel abundant, when a payment notification lands in your inbox.
— You might have a huge fight with a loved one, just before running the best workshop of your career.

How is all of this possible, you ask? You might be thinking to yourself: *The only way for me to succeed is for things to run smoothly all the time, and for me to always feel aligned and unstoppable.*

But that's simply not the case, and to tell yourself that puts limits on what you're actually capable of. You can have a bad day and still run a brilliant seminar. You can feel tired from being up all night with a sick toddler, then run a meeting that leaves everyone feeling energised and empowered. You can feel run-down and uninspired, only for an incredible idea to drop into your mind and heart which turns everything around in an instant.

You can be in alignment when your life isn't perfect. You know why? Because perfection isn't possible anyway, no matter how aligned you are.

Your emotions, mood, energy and desires will fluctuate, shift, change, adapt and evolve. Honouring this truth will allow you to use your life experiences—the positive and the seemingly negative— to create and enhance your ideal life and work.

You are so much more capable than you know. Thinking

you're only capable when you're perfect does a huge disservice to yourself and those you're here to support the most.

So, I want you to think about how you can take the pressure off how you work towards your dreams, to allow yourself to flick the switch on your potentially perfectionistic mindset. You know why?

— Because alignment doesn't mean perfection.
— Because perfectionism is just fear with her prettiest clothes on.
— Because good enough is perfect.
— Because when you try to be perfect, you hide from the people who need you most.
— Because you don't need to be perfect to receive, or serve, or show up, or build something beautiful.
— Because taking imperfect action is better than taking perfect inaction (AKA standing still and doing nothing).

Getting clear to feel clear

Write out a list of all the ways you think you need to be perfect in order to be aligned, take action and receive. Shedding light on this will make it blindingly obvious that it's time to let those perceptions go, and move forwards. For instance:

— *I think that if I'm feeling worried about what my next step will be, I won't ever know what to do.*
— *I think that if my website isn't perfect, no-one will want to work with me.*
— *I think that if my Instagram feed isn't perfectly curated, people will judge me.*
— *I worry that if I don't feel abundant, I'll never make more money.*
— *I'm worried that if I don't feel skinny/tall/pretty/clear-skinned enough, people won't want to hire me.*

— *I'm worried that if I feel anxious or my mood is low, people won't think I'm able to help them.*

— *I'm worried that because I don't always feel inspired, I won't be able to make a living doing what I love.*

Once you have written your list, run yourself through it again. Ask yourself if what you've written is really true, or whether they're just fears you're holding onto, or ways of tricking yourself into thinking you need to be perfect, before you can move ahead in your life and work.

By getting clear on these fears and worries, you can start to clear them away through awareness, with self-compassion and by taking action anyway.

Am I saying you need to purposefully drop the ball and just expect magical things to happen? Not at all. Doing the inner work to feel clear, calm and confident as you build your ideal life is beautiful, important and necessary. I'm simply inviting you to take the pressure of perfectionism off yourself as you do so.

Flipping the mindset

Perfectionism shocks the system into staying stuck and stagnant, which is so very clearly the opposite of aligned and unstoppable. Anyway, aiming to staying stuck and stagnant is not why you're here, right?

How many times have you told yourself that unless you're 100 per cent perfect, you won't be able to call in what you're working on? I've done that way too many times. In fact, I did it just this morning. I was in a funk, and automatically told myself that meant I'd be blocking myself from receiving.

Here's what I did to flip that mindset on its head:

— I grabbed my journal and wrote down what was on my mind, what I had to give up to the Universe, what I wanted support with, and what I felt deeply grateful for.

— I rolled some Frankincense essential oil on my inner wrists, the soles of my feet, my temples, brow and throat chakra area, and over my heart. (I chose this essential oil because it's known to be very grounding and calming, which is how I wanted to feel.)

— I put on some calming, healing chakra balancing music. (I just searched on Spotify for a playlist.)

— I made tea and dipped in a piece of biscotti that my sister had brought over the night before. Yum. I sipped slowly. I brought myself back into the present moment. I reminded myself that everything was okay and on track, and I found myself unravelling and releasing the tension I'd created within.

Perfection is not our aim, it's our mirror

Perfectionism shows us what we must let go of, accept, release, allow ourselves to receive, and what we must move through, to know ourselves more deeply.

Instead of reaching for 'perfect', let yourself do the inner work that allows you to be compassionate and forgiving of yourself; the work that sees you start knowing (and owning) your worth, trusting yourself and your path, and finding your guiding light within.

Do the work you know you're here to do. Allow it to keep evolving, shifting and changing as you do so.

Allow yourself to sit in the space of alchemy, trust and magic. Know that you can still call in what you desire on a 'bad' day, or when you're feeling hormonal, or when you've just had a parking ticket, or when you're feeling stressed or lonely, overwhelmed or puzzled.

While alignment feels like everything is going smoothly and in flow, like things are clicking into place seamlessly and effortlessly, please don't think that life has to be perfect for you to be able to stay in your flow, and continue to move towards your dreams.

Trust your guiding light within

A little while ago, I put one of my guided meditations up on a free meditation website. I was so excited to do this, and felt really proud of the track I'd created and uploaded.

Several hours later, I checked the site and found that several thousand people had already listened to it and left reviews. *Brilliant*, I thought.

Until I started reading the comments on my meditation ...

— A said she loved it and it was going in her favourites.

— D said she found it hard to get used to my voice.

— T said the meditation stopped halfway through, so she didn't enjoy it. (My suggestion would've been to reload the page, but anyway.)

— F said she listened to it before a big meeting, and it helped her a lot.

— My personal fave: B said he liked it but would have preferred it if I didn't sound like I was talking from the bottom of a well! (When I told my mum, she said I should reply with, 'I'm sorry! It's not my fault I live in a well!' Ha!)

— H said it was soothing, empowering and uplifting and she loved it!

— S said I spoke too much, and too fast.

— P said the pace was perfect.

— G said the sound was awful.

— L said the entire meditation was beautiful.

And on and on it went.

I didn't know how to feel or what to think. My heart started to race, my palms went clammy, and my perfectionism swung into dangerous levels. I actually started pacing around my apartment, trying to work out what to do, and how I could make everyone happy.

I read over the positive comments and felt my heart and confidence soar ... then I read over the negative comments and felt myself shrink back, wanting to disappear and delete my meditation from the site immediately.

I felt very attached to the work I'd created, the outcome and the comments. After taking some time away from my laptop and speaking to my husband about it (he gently and kindly reminded me that I could never make everyone happy), I realised had to release myself from the attachment I'd created.

I not only had to allow myself—and my work—to not be perfect, I also had to let others decide for themselves whether they liked my work or not. And perhaps have them decide that it wasn't perfect at all. (Oh, the horror, right?!)

I knew what I had to do. I left the meditation up on the site, and stopped checking the comments.

I took the lesson for what it was: an opportunity to let go of my need to be seen to be perfect; to let myself increase my visibility, even if everyone didn't like what I created or had to say. It was also a chance to clear and balance all of this within myself, before a year where I knew I was going to be in the public eye more, with a couple of really big speaking opportunities that were coming up (including the corporate one I mentioned before, which at the time hadn't yet appeared on my radar).

When things are feeling out of alignment, or when your perfectionism is flaring up, remind yourself that you don't need to be perfect to be in alignment, or to be seen, or to be heard, or to make money, or to love what you do, or to receive. Come back to your body and your breath and to what you've already created.

Let yourself shift out of the tension and attachment to come back into your deeper truth and purpose, your innate worth and enoughness, trusting your guiding light within. You're on the right path, and you'll land beautifully, whether you can see this yet or not.

Lessons in (com)passion

If you could transmute your perfectionism into compassion, what might change for you?

In real time as I write this, the new season of *MasterChef* has just begun (insert hugging/dancing emoji). In one of the episodes, as the pressure builds and the clock ticks, one of the contestants, cooking a delicious-looking Italian seafood stew says, 'I need to cook this perfectly. To do so, I'll do it carefully and with passion.'

I nearly fell off my couch.

Wouldn't it be brilliant if we could all have this attitude next time we want to do something well? Imagine if, instead of letting our negative self-talk punish us into trying to do something with excellence (out of fear of a reckoning), we let ourselves work towards our goals carefully, and with passion (and compassion).

It would settle the doubts, it would calm the fears, it would remove the shakes. It would let us think more clearly, be more rational, stay present and grounded. It would let us do our best work without self-judgement or harm, without punishment or regret.

Of course, we might still buzz with excitement and anticipation; we might still look ahead to the horizon and wonder what the next vista will bring; we might still not be 100 per cent sure that we're doing the right thing—but we'll trust ourselves enough to know that we're doing the best we can, with the skills and knowledge we have today.

An essence for alignment

Another of the Bach flower essences, Rock Water, is wonderful to take here. It's for those who constantly seek perfection, who set rigid goals with high expectations, and who use self-punishment when falling short of these self-created ideals. Rock Water helps you release internal harshness and step back into flow.

ALIGNED AND UNSTOPPABLE AFFIRMATION

I transmute perfectionism into compassion.
I allow myself to be seen exactly as I am. I radiate
my deeper truth and purpose, allowing it to
shine, and I trust my guiding light within.

CHAPTER 11

The Power You Must (Re)claim

I was going through a period where it felt like I'd lost so much of what I'd worked towards for years. Outwardly, nothing was really wrong, but it felt like a sudden (and massive) dip in confidence was blocking almost everything I was working towards from flowing to me.

(The aforementioned perfectionism was impacting on me again here, by tricking my mind into thinking I'd block myself because of the mere fact that I didn't feel confident—a sure-fire way to dampen your confidence even more.)

I did some reflection on the differences between 'now' and 'then'; 'now' obviously referring to how I felt in the present moment and had been feeling for a while, and 'then' how I'd felt (and what I'd allowed myself to receive) in the times when I'd felt more in flow. I noticed three things ...

Firstly, I was viewing the past with this beautiful thing called hindsight, and it was only with hindsight that I could tell myself everything had been completely rosy 'then'. Back then, I'd still had to call on my resilience, find strength when things seemed less than easy, and put myself forwards when I didn't know what the outcome would be. I was comparing two different periods of my life, but conveniently forgetting that while I'd changed and grown in the interim, I had still created that past version, dreamed and set goals and worked towards them (or something better). I'd done it before, and I could do it again.

Secondly, much of my future tripping about how things would never get better was conjecture. I was guessing how things would turn out, while I was planning my very own pity party. Boring. Unhelpful. Also just plain silly.

Thirdly, so much of my outer 'success' (and I define that in terms of how I was feeling within myself and my work, as well as opportunities, visibility, client/workshop attendee numbers, income etc.) had come as a direct result of my inner power. I could see that, years after first truly experiencing this, I was trying to go about things the wrong way.

If I wanted anything to change—and I did—I had to become powerful again, or rather reclaim my power, from the inside first.

I had to let go of self-limiting, victim-based stories, and reprogram my thoughts to support my future self, and my future vision.

What was my next step? Well, like so many make-up products claim to do (and which some do really well—hello illuminator!), I had to let myself glow from the inside out. What does that mean? I had to first radiate that which I wished to call in. I had to radiate my own inner power from the inside out (instead of seeking external validation and thinking it could come from the outside in), no matter what storm I was weathering, no matter what shade of blue (or grey) the sky was.

I could do this by trusting myself and where I was, by trusting I was supported, and by trusting that everything I needed was already within.

This wasn't about denying pain or hard times, but about staying powerful through them, because of them, in spite of them, no matter what.

Resistance to uplevelling

We all go through this from time to time. I find it often comes up when we're stretching, outgrowing the space we've created, the platform we've built for ourselves, when we're being called to go to the next level of our lives. This is your power calling you back to yourself.

It doesn't need to be frightening; it's you, after all. It's the next, bigger version of your life, whispering your name from the other side of the door you're yet to walk through.

Initially, I found myself blustering my way through this phase of uplevelling, even though (on some level) I'd done this many times before, in many different stages of my life and business. But this time it felt bigger. Or perhaps it always feels bigger in the moment; then the mountain recedes to a molehill, as we find our path weaving ahead.

In hindsight, I can see that I resisted this uplevelling for one main reason: I felt that I didn't know how to do it. Ha! What's comical is that we actually always know how to uplevel; we just resist it because of what the uplevelling will mean in our lives.

If you're feeling this resistance too (which can camouflage itself as fear, a sense of stuckness, doubt, overwhelm, limiting beliefs that you know you've worked to clear before, or any number of inner blocks that you could've sworn you'd dealt with already) do this: instead of digging deeper into the problem to find more of the problem (which can sometimes leave you feeling as though you're just digging into sameness), dig deep into your self-enquiry.

Do this to find the healing you need most at that time. Surrender to how you're feeling. Focus on the healing and not the problem. The solution—the uplevelling you need most—will appear for you when the time is right.

That's when we realise we've come up against those inner blocks again to catapult us higher than we've been before. It's when we realise that it doesn't matter if we're feeling fear or stuckness; we can sit in this space, surrender to the unknown and still have dreams that fit us like a glove (but also offer us lots of room to stretch, grow and be pulled towards where we truly need to go).

For me, the healing wasn't about doing anything external, like finding new tasks to tick off, creating new goals to reach, or new heights to climb. It was about climbing that inner mountain of self-doubt, the one that tries to block you from what's next, for the pure and simple fact that you fear the unknown. At such a time, I like to remind myself that I've done this before and I can do it again.

Enquiring with compassion

When enquiring with compassion, you don't berate or punish yourself for not being 'there yet'; you don't wonder why you find yourself in a spot you may have been familiar with just months or years before; and you don't look around and wonder why it seems as though everyone around you is managing so much better than you.

Enquiring with compassion is about gently and kindly asking yourself what you need most right now, in this moment. It's about trusting the timing of what you're creating or releasing. The creativity process is not linear and neither is the process of shedding a skin from your past self.

We have many iterations of ourselves to live and embody

in this life; it makes sense that we should uplevel for each new version of ourselves.

Why do we think this needs to be a linear, perfect, easy and simple process? And why do we think we deserve the roadmap, before we even know the destination of our journey?

Remember that you've done this before, and you can do this again.

You've already uplevelled, because you're here. You've already let go, because you're here. You've already worked towards your dreams, set goals, honoured your intentions and followed your heart, because you're here.

So on some level, you've done this before. But have you done this every single day, all the time? Probably not, because you're human. But still, you're here.

On the way to our next vision, we're allowed to have fear; but let's also have joy and lightness and ease. We're allowed to see our shadows (in fact, I believe we must), but let's make more space for our light.

Don't be scared of how you'll manage a current or even a future challenge. Trust yourself that you'll make it through, because you've done this before, and you can do it again.

Keep radiating what you wish to call in

If you want the relationship, the job, the raise, the promotion, the love, the abundance, the opportunity, the expansion, the momentum ... you have to believe it first. Only then, can you call it (or something better) into your life.

You have to know you're worthy of holding what you're calling in. You have to know you're allowed to receive it. Because it's you—not anyone else—who gives yourself permission to receive.

You might know that I tout the phrase 'or something better' often. So when I say you have to believe it first, I don't mean you have to know the outcome of what you're calling into your life. You don't have to know how it'll happen, or when. But if you want to call something into your life, you have to believe you are worthy of receiving it first. You have to trust there's space within you to receive it, and hold it.

You have to believe you can hold it, and that you're worthy of holding it. Otherwise you may call it in and let it slip between your fingers, before you can even say 'self-sabotage' to yourself.

Sit with this idea for a moment. Place your hands on your heart, and say to yourself: 'I allow myself to receive. What I desire comes from within first.'

Expand before you're ready, to make space to receive

You are always expanding, even when you feel stuck. Hmm, scrap that—especially when you feel stuck. The stuckness is the sense of you pushing out the walls of what's possible for you, because expansion doesn't always have to feel like ease for it to be creating more space in your life.

There'll be another expansion and evolution of you. There'll be another time when you know you're ready for what's next. There'll be another time when you know you're done with what is 'now', even though you have no idea what's coming next.

So let yourself make space now, however you need to, to receive (in) what you're radiating (out).

Trust in the bigger timing at play

We can't control the timing of what we're working towards, but we can always stay in our power with how we approach our dreams, goals and actions.

By trusting that our vision can play out in multiple ways, most of which can't be directly controlled by us, we can allow ourselves the freedom that trust brings.

We can ground our energy down, and deep. Simultaneously, we can hold the space for now, and for new beginnings.

We can call on our resilience, our inner and higher support systems, and trust that we can land with grace, in spite of not knowing the outcome (yet).

ALIGNED AND UNSTOPPABLE AFFIRMATIONS

— *I call my power back to me, reclaiming the power that is always within me.*
— *It's safe for me to lean into the unknown, because I am always guided and supported.*
— *I honour myself and what I need most right now.*
— *I let myself shed and release all I no longer need, making space for who I am and for what's ahead.*
— *It's safe for me to uplevel into what's next.*
— *I am ready to uplevel into what's next.*

CHAPTER 12

Now We Anchor In

There'll always be another level you can reach, another call-and-response to uplevel and upgrade. But your response to that call shouldn't always feel like you're not 'there yet'.

I've been there—to the place where you don't feel 'there yet'—so many times, and it's not the hippest spot in town; it's a place where you don't acknowledge yourself, your hard work, or how far you've come.

Being 'not there yet' is about thinking you're not good enough to be there today; thinking you need more; thinking someone else knows some secret you don't; self-sabotaging yourself with negative, spiralling thoughts, that tell you you're so far away from what you desire.

When we constantly look forward to 'one day', we don't see the beauty of today; the beauty that says our past self would have backflipped to be here today (or, in contrast, that can't believe you're here today and knows that, on some level, you'll get through this).

We want to believe in ourselves to help us reach our dreams, and we're allowed to. We're allowed to believe in ourselves; we're allowed to want more for ourselves; and we're allowed to reach our dreams (or something better).

For each new step we take, for each new level we reach within ourselves, for each time we (re)claim our power, we then need to anchor into it. We can do all the expansion our soul needs, but if we don't anchor into it, we'll never truly feel grounded in our expansion. We'll never truly rise.

When you think about what you're wishing to call in next, do you feel able to hold onto it? And by 'hold', I mean: do you feel able to not just let yourself receive it, but also let yourself make space to keep it?

It might feel uncomfortable

There'll be a time when you must uplevel your work. You'll begin to feel too comfortable within the container you've created; you'll know it's time to adjust, adapt and alter what you're doing, what you're creating.

The process of growing, of creating something new, and of pushing out the boundaries we've previously built for ourselves can feel really uncomfortable—and that's kind of what you want.

When you allow yourself to feel uncomfortable in the process of growth, you allow yourself to grow.

This doesn't mean you have force yourself to do things that don't feel right for you. In fact, it means the opposite. It means you must follow the path of least resistance, which can often take you down the path you initially resisted with all your might.

When we talk about following the path of least resistance, this means to surrender. Surrender to what you can't control, so you can focus on where you can invest your power and energy for the most impact, joy and evolution.

This means you allow yourself to move through a phase of growth that calls on you to feel uncomfortable, albeit for a little while. For soon that stage will feel comfortable too, and your next level will await you.

You'll outgrow your current 'home'; what feels safe, and what feels right. Something new will come to you; something else you must make, or work on, or show up for.

If you hide from the discomfort, you might never experience the joy. And the joy is always worth it.

Make room for more

Imagine taking your own container to a cafe and asking them to fill it with your favourite salad. But when you get there, you realise the container you brought already has food in it. So you might be able to get a small amount of your favourite cafe's salad, but not enough to fill the whole container. You leave feeling conflicted. (Yay for salad!) But did you leave with what you wanted? Or will you just make do with what you have?

To anchor into what you're calling in, you have to make space for what's to come. You have to let go, declutter, reshuffle, release, move on and leave behind things that just aren't serving you anymore, and that won't serve the next level, layer and version of you. You need to make space now, even if you can't yet see what'll rush in to fill the space.

Some ideas to help you do this, coming up next.

Allow the intangible to become tangible

When we're feeling called to go to the next level, we can't always see what the outcome of that will look like. This doesn't mean we can't sense it with all our being; it doesn't mean we aren't crystal clear on what we wish to call in. This is often when overwhelm and a sense of rushing come into play; we can feel and envision what's next, but we simultaneously know we can't control the timing or the exact details.

We have to trust. Allowing the intangible to become tangible is about trusting that you can call in and hold what's next (or something better), without forcing and controlling, but by taking action, dreaming, envisioning and creating. It's about expanding what you believe is possible for you, so that you can expand into this next version of you.

Root to rise

My yoga teachers often say 'root to rise'. They often say this as we're flowing into a pose that requires a balance between grounding down and rising up.

To find this equilibrium, we must be able to root into what we're calling in, as well as rise to meet it. We must ground into this next version through breath and intention, through trust and alignment, through believing in our vision and in ourselves.

Rooting into your vision looks like:
— Believing you're worthy of receiving it.
— Clearing away inner blocks that are holding you back.
— Grounding into your vision before it's materialised in your outer world.
— Trusting you'll know the next best step when the time is right

Rising to meet your vision looks like:
— Taking action, even if you feel uncertain.
— Letting yourself be seen, even if you feel imperfect.
— Trusting you have what it takes, consolidating all you know and all you've experienced, in order to move forwards.

— Letting yourself experience the vision as it is, when it does materialise, instead of controlling or judging it for how it shows up in your life.

Hold that thought within

Have you ever thought to yourself: *When this or that happens, then I'll be more [insert positive attribute]?*

By first holding the thought within, you allow yourself to make space for what you're calling in, even before it has arrived. This sends a message upwards, inwards, outwards and downwards: *I'm ready.*

This calls on you to believe in yourself today; to clear self-sabotaging thoughts first, releasing any remnants of a defeatist attitude that tricks you into thinking the external world needs to change before your inner landscape does (as we discussed earlier).

Anchor your intention with breathwork

You've probably heard this already, but it's paramount to feeling grounded and allowing yourself to expand: breathwork will help you come out of your head, and get back into your body.

When you're in your body, you feel more grounded, peaceful and at ease; you can listen to the wisdom of your body, instead of the panic of your ego; you create a sense of ease that supports your flow, momentum and uplevelling. This helps you feel safe even if (or when) things around you feel shaky, or when uncertainty threatens your sense of forward movement.

It can be as simple as placing one hand on your heart, and one hand on your belly. Then breathe in through your nose, so that you feel the hand on your belly rise. Hold it for a moment or two, breathe out through your nose, hold it for a moment or two, and repeat.

Close your eyes and focus on your breath, being and body. Continue to do this as often as you need.

Do it when you're calling in what's next for you; when you're ready to receive more; when you're releasing and shedding old skins.

Do it when you need to calm your mind and reclaim your power; do it when your mind starts ticking over too quickly; do it when you feel that sense of champing at the bit—wanting to be further ahead, wanting to move faster than you need or ought to.

Integrate what's been, in devotion for what's next

Let yourself integrate and recalibrate, learning lessons and letting go, making space and grounding into your power, truth and alignment. Let yourself integrate the shifts, changes and awareness that each new stage, dream and creation brings to your body, mind and spirit.

When you allow yourself to surrender to this—thanking the energy and vibration of what's already been—you can then anchor into the energy and vibration of what you're calling in. You often have to surrender before you can see tangible evidence of what's coming; that's when you allow yourself to be supported by something greater than yourself.

Allow yourself to expand, rise and ground; expand, rise and ground; expand, rise and ground again.

Everyday ways to support your integration

Here are a handful of easy-to-implement tools you can use to integrate all you've received, learnt and embodied, in order to deepen this in your body, mind and spirit:

— Make time for some gentle journalling on how you want to feel, how you are supporting yourself to feel this way, what you're moving away from or releasing (expectations, fears, worries etc.) and what you wish to embody as you move into the next vision you're anchoring within yourself.

— Enjoy yoga and breathwork, or any kind of mindfulness and meditation that serves you. Sometimes this simply means sitting down with a cup of tea, closing your eyes, placing your hands on your heart, taking a deep breath and tuning back into yourself, allowing energy to shift and insights to drop in.

— Chat to your closest friends about how you're feeling in this stage of life/work/creation. Bounce ideas off each other as to how you can (both) continue to ground your energy and feel supported as you move on. (Ensure you only chat to friends who you know are really supportive, who you don't feel judged by, and who you deeply trust.)

— Pull an oracle card or two and jot down some notes and reflections on how the message of the card/s supports your current situation and the new stage ahead.

— Book yourself in for some body/energy work, which is always a wonderful way to integrate your energy. Kinesiology, reiki, acupuncture, massage and reflexology are high on my go-to list, as is taking time out to treat myself. Manicure, anyone? (A good old nap can do the trick too.)

ALIGNED AND UNSTOPPABLE AFFIRMATIONS

These affirmations will help you anchor into what you're calling in (or what you've already received):

— *I anchor into the present.*
— *I trust in my expansion.*
— *I let myself expand, rise and ground.*
— *I expand my sense of self, to embody the energy I need to call in what's next.*
— *I create space to receive.*
— *It's safe for me to expand into what's next.*
— *I know how to call in what's next.*
— *It's safe for me to call in what's next.*
— *I'm ready for what's next (or something better).*

CHAPTER 13

You're Not a Fraud

When we uplevel into what's next, we have to clear the fears that held us at our prior level. As I've mentioned, these fears might reappear in different versions at each level of ourselves, every time we integrate and recalibrate into what's next. This is to be expected, so judging yourself for it only reiterates a false perception to your body that you're not ready for what's next, when your mind, body, being and soul truly know you are.

If cultivating a positive and resilient mindset is one of the single biggest factors in how you show up to create in your life and business, then believing in yourself is probably at the top of that list.

Staying positive, being resilient, and calling on your inner courage will become your go-to states of being when challenged. You don't need to stumble in times of fear.

Although your stumbling can allow you to create a stronger path forward, how you perceive your situation is up to you. At such times, your self-talk will determine your energy.

Now they all know I'm a fraud

I was being interviewed live for something exciting, that would give me and my business a lot of exposure. I finished the interview feeling on top of the world ... until an hour later, when I realised I'd made a mistake.

Cue: a knot in my stomach, shortness of breath, and a tightness across my chest.

I realised I'd said something incorrect. And while I was confident that it was unlikely most people would pick up on my mistake, I was mortified. My first thoughts went something like this: *I can't believe I said that incorrectly; my mentors and teachers are going to judge me and think I'm not worthy of being here. People will realise I said the wrong thing; but they won't know that I know I made a mistake, so they'll think the whole interview is incorrect and wrong. They won't believe anything I say or write from now on. People are going to think I'm a fraud, and that I have no idea what I'm talking about.*

My hope was that people listening to the interview would give me the benefit of the doubt, and not think it was some horrible mistake that showed how unworthy and fraudulent I was; how much I didn't deserve to be there; how uneducated and inexperienced I really was. (Oh, self-talk can be so intense!)

I sat with those fears for a few minutes. I could feel it about to spiral and become worse, when another (much more calming and grounded) thought landed softly in my mind: *I'm giving myself such a hard time for one tiny mistake ... but am I celebrating all the other things I said in the interview that were right and true?*

Once I realised that I was focusing all my energy in the wrong place and switched my focus to gratitude for what had gone right, I felt my entire body relax. I realised that, of course, this was just a story I was telling myself, and I could change the ending. I swapped the dialogue so that I was celebrating, rather than berating, myself.

I sent a quick email to my interviewer, asking them to please add a little postscript to the audio interview. They agreed, without a moment's hesitation. A little correction to my internal story from my end, led me to ask for a correction to the interview. This meant that I could relax even further into knowing that I wasn't a fraud. I was simply human, and giving myself a very hard time for not being perfect.

You're not a fraud

I have a theory: if you're worried about being a fraud, you are not a fraud.

Fraudsters and charlatans do not worry about being seen as fraudsters or charlatans. They're energised by it, they delight in it. In fact, they probably don't even think they're not being genuine.

What I believe is that if or when you're feeling stressed or worried about being seen or known as a fraud, what's really happening is you're not feeling confident about yourself, your voice, actions, skills, gifts or talents. Perhaps there was a time when you were truly confident about what you were creating or offering, and someone pulled you down because of it? (Witch trials, anyone?)

Answer honestly

I remember when I started working as a nutritionist and naturopath, I was terrified that a client would ask me a question in a session that I wouldn't be able to answer on the spot. Then when it actually happened, I answered honestly: 'Oh, that's such a good question; let me check that for you, and I'll email you after our session.'

Easy. Done. No-one thought I was an impostor naturopath, stealing their time and money and giving them snake oil in return. In fact, my clients appreciated that I didn't try to make up an answer to suit their question; that I was going to invest more time and energy into their treatment, and into finding the best solution for them.

If you're worried you're a fraud or a fake, I have some other ideas about what could be going on for you:

— You're worried that you're not doing enough, whether that's in your life, at home, at work, in a relationship, or for yourself.

— You're worried that you don't know enough in relation to your work and career, to what you're working towards, or in another area of your life that feels deeply meaningful to you.

— You lack confidence in your own abilities (perhaps because you are starting something new and feel like you haven't 'earned' it yet).

— You don't feel safe to speak up and use your voice; this could be at home, at work, online, or within important relationships.

— You've put other people on pedestals (meaning you think they know so much more than you), you're comparing yourself to them, and you're shrinking back because of it.

— You're not celebrating how far you've come, or what you've achieved so far, because you think you still haven't earned the right to celebrate yourself or your achievements.

— You're compartmentalising yourself, not recognising or making use of skills and gifts from your past that easily support what you're doing now.

— You don't feel worthy of success, or of being where you are; this might mean you self-sabotage yourself, play your successes down, or put it all down to luck.
— You're making up stories that people (who?) are judging you out of jealousy, comparison or envy.
— Someone has actually tried to pull you down for being successful and being seen; you haven't forgiven them yet, or detached yourself from the energy of the situation.
— You think you need to keep studying because you don't trust yourself enough yet; you think that maybe another degree will give you the confidence you seek. (Hint: it probably won't.)
— You can't see the wood for the trees. In other words, you can't see a bigger, higher perspective that says: *You're exactly where you're supposed to be, you're doing the right thing, you're on the right track, you're in the right place.*
— You're taking on someone else's story, judgement or criticism, perhaps even holding yourself back out of fear of upsetting or insulting someone you care about.
— You're taking everything incredibly personally and feel co-dependent on external success and validation, always waiting for someone else to pat you on the back, instead of celebrating yourself and owning your achievements, no matter how big or small.

Clearing it out through breath and light

Take a few moments to think about the reasons why you're doubting yourself, and any other possible triggers or underlying reasons about why you're feeling fraudulent or fake.

You may like to journal about this, head to a yoga class, or go for a walk around the block. Let the insights drop in as you need them.

To clear this out, first and foremost I want you to forgive yourself for thinking/feeling/being this way. This is not your forever or your future. It's but a moment in time, when you're being asked to clear away old baggage, align your energy and call your power back to you.

Another way to clear away the old is to write out a list of situations and people you know you must forgive. These may be situations or memories in which you felt small, worried about your place, or as if you were being judged for being a fraud. It may be that certain people make you feel that way (remembering of course, that this is your perception of their perception of you). You don't need to tell the other person you forgive them, unless you feel called to. This is about you releasing energetic ties to old stories, people or situations that are causing you undue stress, holding you back, or taking up your time and energy.

So write out that list, then forgive. Forgive through love, intention, compassion; through simply saying to yourself, *I forgive*. Forgive and set free, however it suits and serves you most. You may like to add some tapping to this too. For example, say: *Even though I don't feel confident in what I'm doing, I deeply and completely love and accept myself*, while tapping specific acupressure points. (Refer to the EFT information in Chapter 8, or search for Emotional Freedom Technique online, to find the specific points to tap.)

Now, place your hands over your heart, your stomach, your throat, your hips, or anywhere else that you feel needs some love, light and attention. Take some deep breaths into that area, filling it with light and love, clearing away old, stuck or negative thoughts or energy, patterns or beliefs, cords or ties holding you back.

See the light expanding upwards and outwards; see your base expand, allowing you to call a fresh perspective and new opportunities and people into your life, to support your journey forwards.

Let yourself build your confidence by taking action: by getting out of your own way; by releasing perfectionism; by not rushing; by giving yourself time to build, grow and experience; by forgiving, loving and trusting yourself.

Let yourself trust your worth, by getting out of your head and coming back into your body.

Trust you are always given what you can handle, and that you're managing this beautifully. Trust that you can always call your energy and your power back to you, which means you can change your own mind, your own story, and your own future.

An essence for alignment

The Bach flower essence of Larch is indicated when you need some support in feeling more confident, especially through speaking up and using your voice, and in taking action to bring about more creative momentum in your life.

ALIGNED AND UNSTOPPABLE AFFIRMATION

I trust myself and what I'm creating and extending out into the world, knowing I'm exactly where I'm supposed to be.

CHAPTER 14

Qualify Yourself

Are you ready to own what you do? Are you ready to acknowledge how far you've come (even if you think you still have places to go), and own where you are, today? Are you ready to claim all the experience you've already lived, all the opportunities you've already created, all the flow and momentum you've already received ... and use all of this to propel you forwards?

Or do you think you still need to do more? Study more? Experience more? Read more? Learn more? Be more of something you feel you're not?

It's important, necessary and enjoyable to continue to learn and grow; but that comes at a cost, if we think we're never 'there yet'. We can do both simultaneously: continually learn and grow, as well as acknowledge where we are and how far we've come.

If you're never able to acknowledge how far you've come, you might find you never think you've learnt enough. You might find you never get to where you want to be. You might find you move the goalposts so much that after a while, there are no more goalposts—just an empty field that stretches further than your eye can see.

While waiting for someone else to give us the go ahead, while thinking we need to ask someone else for permission to go create— and then live—what we dream of for ourselves, we are halting the flow that we so crave and desire. This is the flow that allows us to draw what we desire closer towards us, without the hustle, the burnout, the fear that things –that we—need to be different in order to receive.

If you want to become aligned and unstoppable in your own life, you need to trust that you've made it this far, and that where you are today will take you to where you need to be next. You need to acknowledge your growth and progress (even if the progression feels like a regression at times), and you need to know that you're actually the one and only person who can truly qualify yourself.

I've just had a coaching call with Charlotte, a wonderful client of mine. She'd been questioning her qualifications, wondering if she knew enough, and feeling unsure that her work was enough. Charlotte was doubting her ability to move forwards, because she was only looking at one thing: how many certificates she held in her field. Through a kinesiology balance, we started to shift her energy, mindset and perspective. This helped her see that the papers she held in hand mattered much less than the wisdom, confidence and power she held in her mind, heart and soul.

I know plenty of 'experienced' people who have great qualifications. Does this automatically mean they're empathetic, insightful, creative, driven, grounded and full of generosity of spirit? Ah, no. Does the piece of paper framed in their office or home study generate energy, momentum, opportunities and income? Does it always make them feel energised, aligned and unstoppable? I'd say not.

What does all of that, and more? You do. It's how you feel about yourself; it's your mindset, perspective and self-talk; it's the way you claim where you are and what you do. Ultimately, it's the decision you make to validate yourself, knowing that while there's always more to learn, uncover and discover, you can be satisfied that you know enough for today, while you move forward in your own time.

Here are the goals we energetically aligned Charlotte to:

— I am clear, concise and calm.
— I have clarity about my work.
— I have a clear direction for my next steps.
— I give myself time and space to integrate my ideas, in order to make the best decisions for me.
— I trust the decisions I make.
— I clear my own way.
— I have the confidence to speak up.
— I easily take action on my ideas.
— I allow my Higher Self to lead the way, and I trust that what's going on is divinely guided.
— I trust my Higher Self.
— It's safe for me to step outside my comfort zone.
— I have confidence in what I'm doing.
— I'm confident in myself and in what I'm creating.
— I validate myself.
— I focus my thoughts, to make conscious use of all the wonderful gifts I've received.

From this list of goals, the one that jumps out for me is: *I focus my thoughts, to make conscious use of all the wonderful gifts I've received.*

This is one of the underlying themes of this book. When we focus our thoughts, our energy, our intentions and our actions, then set our sights on honing our voice and using our gifts, we light up ourselves, those we love, and the world.

The stepping stone to doing so is to qualify yourself, validate your own voice, and lean into your uplevelling. Some ways you can qualify—and validate—yourself coming up next.

Invest your energy in the doing, not the deciding

I've seen it all too often: a client finishes one course/certification/degree, only to feel they have to enrol in another, straightaway. Or they start working on a project but spend months in the planning stage, never really taking action to move the dial forwards. Deciding, planning, thinking you need to do more before you let yourself get started—all this can lead you in circles, feeling as if you're chasing your tail.

Sometimes you just have to dive right in. Stop thinking you need to do more; just do what you are waiting to give yourself permission to do.

Decision fatigue is real; so is running around in circles, running yourself into the ground to try to prove your worth, when really, you're already enough.

You'll clear overwhelm when you take action. You'll build your confidence when you move forwards. It's the direct and beautiful opposite of waiting for someone else to pick you, or to validate you.

Clear your own way

We can become so stuck in our own heads when we hold ourselves back, waiting to be validated or chosen by someone else. It's perfectionism, resistance and low self-worth, all tied up in a very expensive bow.

It's expensive because of what it's costing you: the chance to really step up into what's next for you.

So clear your own way by taking action. You're ready to step outside the doorway of this tiny little room you've created for yourself. By being brave enough to say, 'I'm ready, today' you stop boxing yourself in and wondering 'What if?' or saying 'One day ...'. Instead, you open your eyes and see that 'one day' is right now. One day is today.

Lean into your own power

We all have people we look up to in our own line of work. Not surprisingly, if you keep showing up, doing the work you love, pushing your own boundaries and expanding into your greater vision, there'll be a time when people start to look up to you, too.

For this to be true, there must come a time when you claim your inner power back, as well as the ability to lead yourself. In doing so, you become your own leader. Just like becoming your own CEO, this will deepen your self-belief and trust in your ability to create what you want in life and work.

When you qualify and validate yourself, you lean into your power, you radiate what you're calling in, and you let yourself rise to (your own version of) the top.

Use all your experience

You create every day. It's not just 'work' you create—it's your entire life. Becoming aligned and unstoppable in what you create encompasses all the things you invest your time and energy into. So look at the bigger picture; stop compartmentalising everything you've created, and all you've achieved.

Can the lived experience of writing and directing plays at university help you write and create a workshop today?

Can the lived experience of supporting countless friends through heartbreak lift your confidence, as you go through practical clinic hours for your counselling course?

Can helping in your child's school canteen give you the self-belief that you are ready to start that passion project catering company?

If you let yourself open your heart and mind and look around, I'll bet you'll find countless ways your life has led you to exactly where you need to be today.

Trust it's already within you

While you can always learn more, you can also trust that what you need today is already completely within you, and that what you need tomorrow can be called upon when the time is right.

Am I saying you can start calling yourself a doctor with no medical experience? Of course not. I'm merely suggesting you look at all you've already created and achieved in your life, and use all those gifts, skills and experience to allow yourself to start now, to start today—exactly where you are, and with what you already have.

JOURNALLING PROMPT

If you knew and trusted that you didn't need to do more (or be more, or have more), what would you give yourself permission to do right now?

ALIGNED AND UNSTOPPABLE AFFIRMATIONS

— *I trust myself and what I know right now.*
— *It's safe for me to progress and move forward today.*
— *I'm worthy of being a leader.*
— *I'm worthy of being successful.*
— *I'm allowed to be successful.*
— *I celebrate myself and all I've created.*
— *What I'm creating is already within me.*
— *I lean into my uplevelling.*

CHAPTER 15

Step, Step, Pivot

*Don't surrender all your joy for an idea you used to
have about yourself that isn't true anymore.*
CHERYL STRAYED, *BRAVE ENOUGH*

Sometimes we find ourselves far along a path we had desperately wanted to be on, when all of a sudden—or slowly, slowly—we know it's time to move on, to shift, to pivot.

Pivoting can feel terrifying sometimes, especially if we have spent years envisioning ourselves standing exactly where we are, only to find that it's time for something new, a fresh interpretation of our dreams, a new path forwards, and perhaps a shedding of what's already been.

When I left high school, I had no idea what I wanted to do. During a brief stint studying communications and public relations at university (that had me bored and apathetic), I started a make-up course to add some creative joy to my life. I studied make-up in Sydney, followed by Toronto, then started assisting and working in the fashion, beauty and advertising world on my return home.

I did this for several years, until I fell out of love with it. I'll never forget the moment I realised I could change careers and pivot from where I stood: I was on a shoot with a friend who was a stylist, telling her that I wasn't in love with my work anymore. She turned to me and said, 'Well, maybe you won't always be make-upping.' When I think back to that time, my reaction is, *Of course I could change my mind*; but at the time, I hadn't thought like that. I'd worked so hard to get to where I was, so why would I just walk away from it?

However, once the thought was implanted in my mind, an idea started to percolate. Maybe I'd leave my make-up career and study naturopathy and nutrition. As I mentioned earlier, I'd always been interested in the wellness industry. I sat on the idea for a while, until several months later when the Universe nudged me, three times in one week! One day, I was working on a shoot where the model was studying nutrition at the very college I'd been looking into. Then the next day, another model was studying massage at the same college. And then—no joke—the following day, my shoot was at a location just three doors up from that college.

Okay Universe, I hear ya!

Fast forward several years, and I made the shift from working solely as a nutritionist and naturopath, to add in kinesiology. I did so because I needed to, for myself first.

There were so many gifts in being a make-up artist (like getting to be creative with colour every day; meeting new people on shoots; having so much freedom as a freelancer; travelling for work; and developing a strong sense of independence at a young age). And of course, there were many gifts in being a nutritionist and naturopath (such as working with people to support their health; constantly expanding my knowledge in an interesting field; enjoying providing natural treatments to support my clients on so many levels; building my business in my own way; experiencing such joy doing what I loved, and more). But I was starting to crave a different kind of work—one that felt more meaningful for me at that time in my life, more spiritual and more aligned to my evolution, growth and passions.

I had to admit to myself that I was never the clinical nutritionist—I'd much rather read a client's energy and body language than their blood test.

This pivot meant my work shifted organically very quickly. No longer was I seeing clients for digestive issues or hormone imbalances; rather, I was supporting them to find flow when they felt stuck; to feel connected when they felt lost; to remember their worth when they felt 'less than'. Clearing blocks and aligning energy was where I was supposed to be (with some beautiful herbs on the side, if my clients needed them). I knew this was the path for me; I just had to own this new, deeper truth.

Soon after I added kinesiology into my business it boomed; I became fully booked for a couple of months in advance. My clientele also shifted, and I started attracting healers, coaches, creatives, entrepreneurs and small business owners. I supported them in mind, body and spirit work, as they built deeply aligned lives and businesses. I knew—more than ever—that this was my true purpose in my work.

However, even though I'd craved and worked towards this change for so long, knowing deep down that this needed to happen for my highest evolution and growth, I also felt some resistance to this change in my business. Surprisingly, it wasn't so much at the beginning of the pivoting, as when it started to feel like I was really making strides with the change.

You know that feeling when things start to go really, really well, and we wonder when the other shoe will drop? Perhaps we feel like it's a fluke, a fleeting moment in time when things feel aligned and expansive, when those feelings of fear and resistance pop up to sabotage us in our tracks.

It felt like it started outside of me, and filtered through when I felt like I had to justify the shifts and changes in my business. But in truth, it was coming from within, sown from the seeds of my own self-doubt. This was simply a reflection of my own energy, mindset and fears.

It continued when I wondered if I was communicating properly about my work. Months and even years later, people would still refer clients to me for naturopathic issues, when my main work had shifted away from that. It reached boiling point within me when people asked how my 'nutrition business' was going—when I hadn't done a nutrition consult in five or six years. (Hilariously, and as if to remind me of it while writing this chapter, it happened again just last week.)

Your pivot is your expansion

I think of pivoting as another version of expanding. Sometimes the fear I held around this change, shift and expansion wasn't something I'd created; rather, it was something that had been reflected onto me, that I'd absorbed as truth.

I can pinpoint when this might've happened, at least in part. Years before, I'd talked to a fellow female business owner who'd made a less than positive comment about a coach who'd changed track, from coaching in the health and wellness world to business coaching. She'd joked that 'failed health coaches' often turn to business coaching.

That comment stuck with me, more than I'd have liked it to, and in the back of my mind it didn't sit right with me. It felt judgemental, reductive, small-minded, and even gossipy. It gave me an underlying worry that I too would be judged as a 'failed naturopath' whenever I told someone about the new path I was taking in my life and business; rather than letting it be seen for what it truly was: a woman trying to do her best work in the world, following what lights her up the most.

I continued to work on this within myself—to trust myself to follow what was lighting me up; to love what I was creating; and to back myself all the way. When people who didn't follow my work asked me about my nutrition business, I consciously decided to stop feeling triggered, and I simply explained what I was doing, grounding and anchoring both myself and the energy around me in this reality, radiating it out for all to feel, see and experience.

Own your truth

If you constantly look for validation from others to move forwards, you'll create situations where you need the approval of others to do so. To become aligned and unstoppable in your work and life, you have to be aligned and unstoppable in your truth; in what calls to you, what lights you up, what lifts you up, and what makes you feel purposeful, driven and devoted.

You can't play small to fit a mould set by someone else, and you certainly can't keep going down a path that doesn't fit you anymore. That'll only end in apathy, exhaustion, tears, resentment, and a deep daily drag in your bones; an emptiness in your heart because you know you have so much more to give. You have to let yourself pivot, own your truth and by doing so, step even more deeply and fully into alignment.

The best decision

One day, just before writing this book, I received the following email from Aimee, a lovely client of mine. It helped me see that my pivoting had been the absolute best decision I could've made; for myself, my work, my life, and for those I wish to serve most.

> Dear Cassie,
>
> I've just read your blog post about trusting the 'enoughness' of my business, and thought I'd drop you a wee note to say that, ever since you 'pivoted' towards business coaching, I have been absolutely loving virtually everything you've released! I rewatch bits of the Love What You Create training almost weekly. Between the Love What You Create Workshop, the Facebook lives, and the Beautiful Business webinars, it's like I have on-demand access to this incredibly reassuring and encouraging library of your videos, for when I need a pick-me-up on my entrepreneurial journey.
>
> I actually chuckle to myself whenever I download a freebie, see your beautiful sales funnel and go, 'Yup, already got that', 'Yup, already got that too'! Haha.
>
> So I just wanted to say thank you for not just 'teaching' me how to release some of those things that weigh us down, but leading by example and actually taking me through a process of growth and deep alignment with what I am doing in my biz.
>
> All the best with the exciting new things that are in your works, and I look forward to the next Mastermind! =)
>
> A

That is an email to make your day (or week)! You see, I'd been doing this work for years—but at times, there was still a part of me that felt almost ashamed to really, truly own it, for fear of upsetting the people who perhaps wouldn't benefit from my work, instead of leaning into deeply supporting those who would.

I now knew I had to take not just a teaspoon of my own medicine, but the whole glorious bottle. And then make more bottles to both sell on and continue taking myself! Taking a bottle of my own medicine meant finally, deeply, truly acknowledging not just what lights me up, but honouring that it helps light the way for others too.

There's no point keeping yourself stuck on a path that doesn't fuel you anymore, in the blind hope that you're still supporting others, while tricking yourself into thinking there can't be another way forwards.

We've all had the experience of working with someone who is clearly not aligned to their work—someone who wishes they could pivot, sidestep, course-correct or change direction. There's the snappy waitress who wants to quit and start a fashion degree; the bored plumber who wishes he could open a cafe; the tired receptionist who wants to become a teacher.

Long gone are the days where we have one career for our whole life. If we believe we can follow our dreams, we also have to believe that our dreams can follow us.

So next time you feel your dream following you, tugging at you, tapping you on the shoulder, please turn around. Look into its big eyes and acknowledge it; tell it you're coming, and then course-correct, pivot, change your mind ... and chase it!

Following bliss

And so it was that when reading Aimee's email, I realised (again!) that by following my bliss, I'm helping others follow theirs. I realised that this is the work I must teach, because it's the work that fuels me the most; trying to hide what makes me feel the most seen is not how I want to live, to feel, to be.

If there's something you're being called to do and you don't teach it, live it, embody it or share it, then the person you'll be dishonouring most will be yourself.

Know this: the world doesn't need the bitter, resentful, hardened version of you. The world needs the you that's lit up and on purpose, embodying your gifts and your creativity. That's the version of myself that I want to be. How about you?

Pivoting, with fear and all

There is a middle path, but it goes in only one direction: toward the light. Your light. The one that goes blink, blink, blink inside your chest when you know what you're doing is right.

Cheryl Strayed, *Brave Enough*

Sometimes when we're called to course-correct, our fears try to take the lead. This is when we must go deeper, listen to our truth, lean into our light and course-correct; pivot, shift, release, change our minds and then show up, anyway.

Even if you're unsure of the outcome. Even if you're worried that no-one will like your decision. Even if you think they'll judge you. Even if you think they'll talk behind your back, or laugh in your face.

To pivot even when you're fearful is to visualise what you're creating and to hold it within your sights, even before you've taken a step forwards. It's to take the first step, even though you have no idea where your foot will land, whether your heart will carry you all the way, and whether you're brave enough to keep walking without the map you thought you were following.

The truth is, there is no map. There is only you, following what lights you up, putting your fears to bed by clearing them away (or acknowledging them and moving forwards anyway); reminding yourself, every single day, that you're worthy of creating this, of showing up, of being seen, of being heard, of speaking up.

And even though at times you might not remember that, remember this: we need your light, your voice, and your work, and if you let fear get in the way, we'll simply never know what you could've created... had you known you are enough.

Your work is needed in this world. Your light is needed, every day, all the time, now more than ever.

Follow the fear but don't let it lead you

You can follow your fears for a while, those fears that say, 'Don't pivot! Don't change! Don't do something new!' But there'll come a day (or rather many days, many times, many moments) when you'll have to take the lead; when you'll have to clear away your fears and move forwards anyway.

Fear can only lead you so far. Then your courage, drive, determination, purpose and passion must take over.

I have mixed feelings about the idea that we should always let fear lead us. Sometimes, yes. Sometimes fear is simply an anticipation of doing something we've never done before; those nerves before speaking at an event; the palpable sensation of knowing you have no idea how it will go, but you feel called to do it anyway. Sometimes fear is protecting you in a way, even though you don't need protection; and yes, sometimes you must 'feel the fear and do it anyway'.

But if you only do things out of fear, from fear, in fear of fear, you're not living in the present moment; you're not grounded in your body; you're not clearing away what's holding you back; you're not fully connected to the wellspring of support and guidance that's always available to you—the support and guidance that comes from your intuition, your inner self, your Higher Self, the Universe and your Guides.

If you only ever take action from a space of fear, you're not feeling the joy and connection, the flow and ease, that comes from taking action in alignment. When you take action from a place of alignment, fear will sometimes pop up, of course. But the trust feels stronger. The grounding is there. You have a strong base. You're following what lights you up. Your foundations are rooted in place and this supports what you do next.

So please, allow yourself to listen to your fears, but tune into a deeper level too. Let yourself be guided by fears that need love and attention, and fears that need to be transformed into something that'll support your next step.

Listen to your fear, but listen to your light first. Your fear might suggest you stay exactly where you are, on the path you've been walking for years; but your light will guide you to take the next best steps for you, fears and all.

Give yourself the permission you're craving

To my business owner clients, I always say: 'It's your business, and your choice.'

I say this because, well, it's your business/art/work/career/ path/purpose—so it's your choice! This means you get to choose (yes, really) how you show up for yourself, and how you show up for others. This means you get to change your mind:

— If something isn't working for you, you get to let it go.
— If something feels stuck you can shift it, so it brings in more flow.
— If you don't love something anymore, you can let it go (with love).
— If things are feeling complicated, you can simplify them.
— If you're feeling exhausted, you can decide to rest.

I could go on, but none of what I write here will mean anything unless (and until) you give yourself permission to change your mind ... and do the work that lights you up the most.

Intuition is your strategy

While we're talking about the inner side to this beautiful work, let's talk about intuition. Intuition is the one strategy I can always rely on; the one that always delivers; and the one that promises to help you build, expand and maintain a creative life and path that's deeply aligned to who you are.

Building your creative life and path based on your intuition means making decisions that might not 'sound right' to other people, but that feel so right for you. It means creating that which feels deeply aligned to who you are, without having to look around at what everyone else is doing.

It means knowing how to move forwards when you need to; pulling back from work when you know you need a break; making decisions when intuitive hits come through; and not worrying about any external hype that sometimes filters through, because you know how to receive—and then utilise—the intuitive information that comes through you, to you and for you.

Intuitive decisions might not always make practical sense; but on the flip side, an intuitive decision feels right and sounds right. The time to really tune into your self-belief and back yourself is when the decision you're making is the one that feels the most expansive, and the most aligned to the greater vision you hold for yourself (even if you now have to dream up something entirely new).

How do you start listening to your intuition? You slow down and tune out the noise from outside. You come back to your breath, your sense, your self. You let yourself open up to receive guidance and you let yourself trust it. Although all the puzzle pieces might not fit just yet, you trust that the bigger picture will become clear in time.

Are you getting an intuitive nudge about something? Are you listening? Listening to it can feel simultaneously expansive and slightly intimidating (because it can mean your uplevelling is imminent). I find that when the opposite happens (not listening to your intuition), it feels like trying to see through the energetic version of that white claggy glue we used to use in kindergarten. I'd pick an intuitive jump into the unknown that feels equally expansive and intimidating—over staying stuck and stagnant—any day.

Own your truth and pivot when you need to

— Follow what lights you up.
— Believe in yourself and the new the path you're carving out for yourself. No more second-guessing yourself.
— Let yourself take risks. Be unashamed of the fact that you're ready for something different, something more, something new.
— Let go of how you think others perceive you. Use that energy to fire up your self-belief, and to fuel your own passions and purpose instead.

An essence for alignment

For extra energetic support in pivoting and transitioning, take the Bach flower essence of Walnut. It'll help you let go of thinking about what other people might believe, and help you stay true to your own path, goals and dreams.

ALIGNED AND UNSTOPPABLE AFFIRMATIONS

— *I give myself permission to do the work that lights me up the most.*

— *It's safe for me to change my mind.*

— *I let myself pivot, following the direction of my highest self.*

— *I trust I'm being guided onto the best path for me.*

— *I'm allowed to shine.*

— *I'm allowed to do the work I love.*

— *I trust myself and my intuition.*

— *I allow the bigger picture to become clear, all in good time.*

— *It's safe and easy for me to listen to, and trust, my intuition.*

— *I know how to trust my intuition.*

— *I easily use my intuition and guidance to support and direct me.*

— *I believe in myself and what I'm creating next.*

CHAPTER 16

Honour Your Soul Work

It was late on a Saturday afternoon and I'd just returned to my hotel in Melbourne, after running the first of four writing workshops I was holding around Australia.

I sat on my bed, energy coursing through my veins, my breath steady, my eyes bright, and I promptly burst into tears. *This is what I'm meant to be doing,* I thought to myself. *This!*

Never before had I felt so connected to my work, purpose and vision. I thought back to the morning; just hours before, I'd been in the same hotel room, feeling an intense mix of excitement, anticipation, tingles of fear and a deep drive and devotion to my dreams. And now, I'd done it. I'd done something new, expansive and so powefully on soul purpose that I thought I might burst with joy.

And all of it was only possible because I'd let myself pivot to honour my soul work.

Be known for the work you love doing

When we allow ourselves to pivot, we allow ourselves to honour our soul work. Especially when that means saying 'no' to opportunities our past selves would have done a backflip for.

One morning I was sitting at my desk, waiting for a client to arrive. I received an email from a journalist, asking if I'd like to come on TV to speak about the dangers of eating bad fats, and how to incorporate more good fats into your diet.

I wanted to say 'yes' so badly ... but I couldn't. It had been years since I'd stopped focusing on nutrition and health in that way. Not only would I have had to brush up on my knowledge in order to be interviewed on television, I didn't want my first TV appearance to be focused on something I was not passionate about and no longer focused on in my work.

I thought to myself: *If I do this interview and it grows from there, I'll start to become known for something I don't love. I'll start to be thought of as 'that woman who spoke about trans fats on TV' and that's not at all what I want.*

So I declined. But first, I mulled it over for a full day. Declining a live national TV interview was hard to do; as soon as I sent off my reply, I almost regretted it. But I knew that saying 'no' would keep the path clear for when I felt called to say 'yes'—and for where I wanted to go.

Fast forward several years, and my first television appearance was to promote my second book. Now, that's something I'm proud of. That's something I truly wanted to do. That was something worth waiting for. And it was made possible because of the path I carved out for myself; the path that included saying 'no' when asked to appear on live national television on a Sunday night.

Had I let fear, lack or ego jump in, I would have said 'yes'—out of a fear that saying no' would ruin something for me, or that I'd upset the journalist; out of a sense of lack, that this might be my only chance to go on television to talk about my work; out of ego, thinking I should say 'yes' simply because I was asked to do something so big and exciting.

But I said 'no', because I wanted to be known for the work I loved doing the most.

Stop doing the work you don't love

Writing about food, health and nutrition was how I got my start writing media articles; my first-ever published article was in a weekly tabloid magazine, and it was about five foods to eat to ease bloating. Initially, I was overjoyed to be doing that work.

The requests started to roll in, and I was soon writing articles, commenting or providing quotes almost every week. This went on for several years, until the shift in my work. For quite a while after my shift from nutrition and naturopathy, into kinesiology and alignment work, I continued to receive requests from freelance writers, various media outlets and websites, asking for my comments on topics like *The Top 10 Non-Dairy Nut Milks* and *18 Superfoods You Must Eat Today*.

To be honest, while I was still grateful to be on the radar of these writers and websites, I started to feel resentful when these emails arrived. I knew I had to start saying 'no', and by doing so, open up new doors for myself.

I found that if I was open and honest about the changes, it sparked new insights and conversations; I could feel content, knowing that I'd told one more person about my soul work.

I spoke up

My body would tense up when I'd receive yet another email asking for my opinion on non-dairy nut milks. It came to a head one day, when I received an urgent (so urgent!) email, asking for my comment about ... kale. The journalist needed my response within the hour. My jaw tensed, and I almost threw my empty tea-stained mug across my desk. My physical response, my body's answer, was a complete, resolute, absolute refusal. It was not my soul work any longer and I had to honour that, or my resentment would continue to bubble up (and one day I might actually break my mug).

I also knew that if I didn't start to speak up about my current work, I'd continue to receive emails asking me to write about almond milk and kale. (Side note: I love almond milk and kale, I just don't love writing about them.)

So I took a deep breath. I centred myself. I sent gratitude and love to this woman, because I was indeed so grateful to be thought of, and I replied like this:

Hey V,
Thank you so much for getting in touch! I'm grateful you thought of me for this piece.

Lately my focus has shifted, and I no longer write about food and nutrition. If you're working on any articles or stories about any of the following topics, I'd love to be considered for an interview, comment or article:
- Creativity, writing, and loving what you create
- Business coaching with heart and soul
- Energy and emotions
- Life and business alignment work
- Self-love and self-care
- Self-worth and comparison
- Trust and intuition

I'd also love to introduce you to D who's a nutritionist. I'm sure she would love to help you out with the article you're working on now.

Thank you again, and I look forward to working together on another piece soon.

Cassie x

Go ahead

There'll be times we need to say 'no' to old soul work, in order to bring in the new. And when the 'new' feels so close you could reach out and grab it? That's when we'll need to step up, once more honouring this season of our soul work, making space for ourselves, and celebrating what we love to do.

I recently received an email from an old client of mine, Mia, who was releasing a new product that had a similar name to one of my offerings. She was worried I'd be upset or think she was copying me; but she was also proud of what she'd created and really wanted to go ahead with her launch.

I didn't need a moment to think about my reply. Here it is:

Hey Mia,
Thank you so much for getting in touch, and for your lovely email.

Please launch your offering! I so appreciate you letting me know, thank you. My books have the same name as many other books. I definitely feel more than okay with us having same/similar names for products. I also know that when we create our own soul work, it's always unique to us—no matter if it has a similar name to another product. Good work always has a place.

Thank you again for reaching out. I really appreciate it.

Hope all is well, and big love right back,
Cass xxx

There is space for all of us.

There can be so much fear around creating and releasing our own work, when you wonder if it's enough. There can be times when you wonder if your work will be judged because it's similar to the work of others, or even too different.

What I've come to understand is that when we create our own soul work, it's always unique to us—no matter if it has a similar theme or even a similar name to another product.

This doesn't give you a free pass to plagiarise the work of others with just a tiny twist; you must still do work that is honest and unique to you. And if your work is good and real and true (to you), your work will be found. It might be found by one person, or by thousands, but it'll be found.

This doesn't mean you won't have to show up for yourself and your dreams; this doesn't mean you won't have to speak up about yourself, your work, and your gifts; and it certainly doesn't mean you'll never feel a fear of failure, uncertainty or self-doubt again. But it does allow you to know that if you keep showing up, creating and releasing your work, letting yourself be seen and heard, it'll get found.

The way to do that is to create good work. And really, the only way to create good work is to create your soul work.

Creating and honouring your soul work

When you create your soul work, you are honouring the part of you who needs this self-expression the most.

What's your soul work? It's the work that lights you up, from deep inside, from high above, from down below. It lights you up from every angle, with every perspective giving you a clear view right into your soul. It's the work you must do; it's the work that calls you to it; it's the work that fills you up; it's the work that is you—without being attached to you.

It's the work that only you can do.

You might not be clear on how to find and follow your soul work yet, and that's okay. If that's the case, I suggest you:

— Don't overthink it

Most things become saturated with confusion when we overthink them. So please don't overthink your soul work. Your soul isn't overthinking it, so why do you need to?

— Keep showing up

Keep making space to conjure and dream, to evoke and create, to brainstorm and map, and to feel into what you're wanting to make. It doesn't matter if you start and stop, start and stop, while you're working out what works for you. Because the only way you'll find it is to make space to see it.

— Keep following what lights you up

Listen to the whispers that guide you in the right direction. They're easiest to listen to when it's quiet, and when you're not forcing or rushing. So make some space to sit with yourself, or some time to work it out, and keep following the intuitive nudges that guide you in the direction of your dreams (even if they don't make complete sense).

— Course-correct

Course-correcting is how we simultaneously embody alignment and invite more of it in, when we feel off track. If you find yourself along the path of doing your soul work but something starts to feel off, or out of whack, or not in alignment with your energy and dreams, you have full and complete permission to let it go. Readjust your perception so it's focused on what feels best for you, instead of holding onto an old dream.

JOURNALLING PROMPT

What would honouring your soul work really look like?

ALIGNED AND UNSTOPPABLE AFFIRMATION

I give myself permission to do my soul's deepest work. It is safe for me to follow what lights me up, to let myself do the work I love the most, and to follow the intuitive nudges of my dreams, guidance and intuition.

CHAPTER 17

Listen ... But Not to Everyone

I once went to see an energy healer I really trusted and looked up to. I'd been on a real roll in my business; after years of hard work, it felt like things were starting to pay off for me. I was relishing all the opportunities, wonderful clients and money I'd spent years making space for—and was now allowing myself to receive—in my life and business.

I'd been working on a big new project and was about to launch it. I went to see this practitioner for support prior to the launch; but after the session, I really wished I hadn't.

Let me explain something first. Kinesiology is energy and alignment work—it's not a tool to foretell the future. If you want to work towards something, but a block might be holding you back, we can work to clear it, align your energy, and change your thought patterns. This in turn can change your actions and help you come back into alignment, so that you can move forwards with more ease and flow, always helping you stay connected to yourself, your source of power, and your free will.

With the kind of kinesiology alignment work I do, if a client comes to me with a goal—whether it's a personal goal, or a business, career or work goal, or anything else they're working towards—my intention is always to support them to clear their own way, shift out of negative patterns, and deepen their self-trust and self-confidence, to allow themselves to reach their goals (or something better).

They can then take action from a place of confidence. They can make the changes that'll make all the difference. They can let go, move forwards, lean into what they desire—they can feel free to expand into the best version of themselves.

If the outcomes of their goals don't go to (their) plan, we work on acceptance of that, course-correct, ground their energy, and carry on. If things turn out better than expected, we celebrate.

But I never, ever, ever tell a client they can't reach their goals. I never look them in the eye and tell them their dreams and goals just won't happen, or tell them to aim lower.

This is exactly what the energy healer did to me, one sunny morning in March, many years ago.

At the start of the session I explained where I was at: my current focus and goal with my work; what felt like it was working really well; and what felt a little out of alignment or stuck. I was excited about where I was at with my work, and my anticipation for the coming launch was palpable. All the content and tech side of things were ready to go—I'd been working on it solidly for months.

The last piece was my mindset, to ensure I was ready to go, open and willing to let in a whole new round of amazing clients, hold the space for them, and facilitate a wonderful course and experience.

When I told the practitioner my goal, within just a few moments I was told it wouldn't happen. The practitioner didn't 'feel' I'd reach that goal this time ... but maybe next time. I was asked to consider a lower goal I thought I might be able to reach.

Um, what? My first thought was, *But this is energy work ... you're not telling my future. The point of this session is to clear the blocks so I can work towards my goal, not add more blocks to my path and tell me I'll never get there anyway.*

I honestly can't remember much more of that session; I probably shut off because I stopped trusting the practitioner. At the end of the session, when it was suggested I come again, I'm pretty sure the look on my face conveyed my reply. *Thanks, but that'll be a 'no' from me.*

I got into my car in tears and called a girlfriend. This was so against how I practised and what I believed; it felt like a physical, mental, emotional and spiritual affront (which, in a way, it was).

Then I had to get back to working on my launch, while also undoing all the 'work' this energy healer had tried to do in our session. I did kinesiology balances on myself. I cleared my energy, the energy of my office, and booked a clearing and coaching session with a healer and girlfriend I trusted.

I went to yoga, and journalled pages and pages about how angry and upset I was because of the session. It felt like a waste of time and money, but mostly a waste of my energy. I had known and trusted this person, and they'd very consciously (or perhaps subconsciously) tried to pull me down.

This wasn't what I wanted to be doing with my time, just before a launch, but it was so important to me. I didn't want to go into the launch carrying remnants of someone else's negative story, pattern or pushback.

It took me a really long time to let go of that practitioner's words; their doubt in me and my ability, or rather their choice to not support me in clearing a block that might have come up in relation to reaching my goal.

While I didn't reach the initial goal I'd set, it was still my most successful launch at that time. I was incredibly proud of myself, naysayer and all.

What I learnt from that experience served me well:

— Don't take it on

There'll always be people who say negative things about your work, your goals, or your dreams. And you can listen, without taking them on.

A close girlfriend and healer taught me to say 'thanks, no thanks' to myself, when confronted with thoughts (your own, or someone else's) that don't feel quite right for you. It works a treat.

— Set more goals

When I set goals now, I set several. No longer do I simply look ahead to one goal, but to many. Then as I hit milestones on the way to my stretchiest goal, I get to celebrate every step of the way. It also means that if I only hit the first goal, or one version of my goal, I've still hit a goal. And even if I don't totally reach that goal, I'm still okay.

I also like to set myself little rewards along the way. When I hit my first goal, I might give myself a slow morning off in my favourite cafe, reading and drinking coffee. When I reach my second goal, I might buy myself a new plant for my office (like I need an excuse!). Third goal? A one-hour massage. Fourth goal? Dinner at my favourite restaurant with hubby.

You could also give your goals names, like 'stretch goal', 'stretchier goal' and 'stretchiest goal'; or emotive feelings, like 'abundant goal #1', 'aligned goal #2', 'dreamy goal #3' and so on.

When writing down my goals, I always end with a little plus sign, as a way of saying, 'This is what I'm aligning myself to ... or something better'. Sometimes I'll simply write, ... *or something better* at the end of the goal.

Make it fun, enjoy the process, stay in your power, work with people you trust. Most importantly, trust yourself first.

— *Your power is yours*

One of the reasons I felt so deflated after that 'healing' session is because I'd put this person on a pedestal, so I allowed them to govern my energy. I thought they knew better than I did, so I gave away my power.

You can ask for and receive help and support on your journey, without giving away your power. You always have the power to listen to your intuition and use it as a powerful tool to help you navigate your next steps. If something feels off, honour that feeling. Of course there are times when we feel so vulnerable that any advice seems like good advice. That is when it's best to not rush into action; let the advice simmer within, and then trust that the right answer—your right answer—will appear for you.

Listen to yourself too. You can ask for support, but don't stop listening to your own inner guidance system. Remember ... take what you need, and leave the rest.

Crystals for alignment

Some of my favourite crystals to help you feel centred, grounded and protected are:

— **Amethyst**: calming and protective, it helps you feel clear on your own intuition and vision.

— **Black tourmaline**: for protection, especially great when you need to strengthen your boundaries and clear away negative energies.

— **Clear quartz**: a master healing crystal, it opens and activates your ability to receive clear guidance, clears away energy blockages, amplifies your positive intentions and supports clarity of mind.

— **Hematite**: another powerfully protective stone, it grounds your energy, transmutes negative energies, and helps you feel focused and centred.

— **Rose quartz**: a wonderful crystal to work with to support self-love and acceptance, forgiveness and compassion. Useful when you need to do some forgiveness work, in relation to any situation that supports you in deepening your love and compassion for yourself and others.

A note about working with crystals

I'm hesitant to offer you any advice or support that sees you put your power in anyone else's hands, and that includes working with crystals.

Think of it this way: if you pick up a rose quartz, will it automatically bring more love into your life? Hmm perhaps, but more likely, it'll simply be a tool—one of many—in your toolkit to help you radiate that which you wish to call in. Working with crystals may help you set clear intentions, which helps you take aligned action, which helps you move forwards in the best way possible.

Use crystals as a tool to support you, not as a crutch to catch you.

ALIGNED AND UNSTOPPABLE AFFIRMATION

I stay within my centre and source of power, always listening to and trusting my intuition and guidance, as I work towards my goals in life and work.

CHAPTER 18

Acknowledging the Roller-Coaster

By now, I think we'd all agree that working towards what you want in life and work sometimes feels like a roller-coaster. It doesn't much matter whether you're on the 'creative' or 'business' ride, life itself has so many ups and downs. And never more so than when it feels like your livelihood (and sometimes, your happiness) depends on your work, self-expression and creative energy.

There are the huge 'ups' when things work out well, like when you launch something new that's taken up well by those around you; when your hard work pays off; and when things work out as you'd hoped (or even better).

There are the exhilarating rushes when amazing opportunities land in your lap, seemingly out of nowhere (except that, of course, it's through your hard work for many weeks, months and years prior that's drawn the opportunities towards you).

There are the deeply satisfying times when you feel so connected to your work, so incredibly on track, unshakable in your self-esteem, self-worth, passion and purpose; the times you can't imagine doing anything else except what you're doing right now; the times you feel so buoyed up by your work, your dreams, your goals.

And then ...

There are the times you feel whacked by your perceptions, your expectations, and by the things that don't go to plan; the times you wonder how you'll actually keep moving forwards, when everything feels so hard, so out of reach.

There are the steep 'downs' when it feels as though nothing is working, flowing or moving as you'd like/anticipated/dreamed/schemed.

There are the times you make up stories about everyone else's success; when it seems that everyone is doing so much better than you are; when you dig yourself deeper into your fear-based misgivings, feeling like you're missing something that everyone else understands.

I've been running my own business since 2011. Except for a short time when studying at make-up colleges in Sydney and Toronto (when I worked at two huge, global make-up megastores that you probably know and love), I've worked as a freelancer or been self-employed for my whole adult life. This means I know a thing or two (or seven million) about the ups and downs of creative, purposeful, soul-based work, which can sometimes look like you earning money from what you create. Of course, this is why I continue to both teach this work and deepen it within myself.

If you're here, it might be because you've decided to step off the roller-coaster that the purpose-based, creative, entrepreneurial life can be.

I know that roller-coaster. I know what the 'ups' feel like (exhilarating); I know what the 'downs' feel like (crushing); I know what the cruising feels like ('I could get used to this').

I know what it feels like when you buy your ticket for this ride. The anticipation feels palpable, when you take that first step onto the roller-coaster and you tell yourself that this is where you're supposed to be (because it is). You sit down, buckle your seatbelt, look around you and think, 'Yes, I'm doing this!'

Then the ride starts, and you feel yourself climbing ... higher and higher, and it's all you ever wanted. You tell yourself you'll never fall, you'll never feel the dips, you'll never stop rising. Everything will be okay.

And then it happens. The atmosphere changes, the angle of your seat shifts, and things feel very different all of a sudden. You don't know what happened or what changed. Weren't you just climbing? It felt so wonderful to be going so high. Did you do something wrong? Is everything still okay?

And then you realise ... you bought the ticket for the biggest roller-coaster ride of them all, and this is what happens on that particular roller-coaster. We go up, and then down, and then we might cruise along for a little while, before rising and falling and rising and falling again.

Getting off that roller-coaster

See? I told you I know how that ride feels. I also know what it's like to ask to get off.

We get off the roller-coaster of our creative life:
— when we decide that rising is made possible because of our falls.
— by raising our standards, and by allowing ourselves to ask for more.
— by trusting ourselves, forgiving ourselves for having self-sabotaging thoughts, and letting ourselves receive as much as we give.

— by bringing our fears to the surface so we can clear them.
— by deciding that 'good enough' is better than procrastinating and not making (or releasing) anything at all.
— when we decide that enough is enough, because we know that we are enough, today.
— when we honour our own flow; the natural rhythms and cycles of our body, energy, and creativity.
— and lastly, when we realise that the ups and downs are all part of life, knowing that we can surrender to each of them in turn, supporting ourselves along the way.

We all know that acknowledging and accepting where we are (and what's not working) is the first step to changing anything. So we'll do that first, here and now. It's also important to see the 'downs' of the roller-coaster as not necessarily bad, and the 'ups' as not necessarily good. They are all part of the ride to becoming aligned and unstoppable in your life and work.

I want you to think about how you're currently feeling about your creativity, self-expression, work, path, purpose, career and/or business. I want you to start getting clear on how big your ups and downs feel, and what is fuelling and triggering them.

The opposite of sky-high ups and rock-bottom downs isn't a flat, boring road that feels like it's taking you nowhere. Far from it. Nor is it the feeling of only climbing higher and higher. We need our shadow as much as we need our light. We need our shadow to have a sense of our light, and vice versa. We truly aren't one without the other. We need to feel the downs and the 'failures', to know what our own version of success looks and feels like.

You wouldn't want a roller-coaster that only climbs up. It's not that it would become boring (although, that's possible); it's because very often, your shadows and your failures and your challenging times create the foundations on which you build your most brilliant, bold, courageous self.

Here are some questions for you to answer:

— What does your roller-coaster currently feel like? (e.g. ungrounded, uncertain, out of your depth, confused, overwhelmed, lacking in self-trust/confidence/belief, stuck in lack, scared or fearful)

— How would you prefer to feel? (e.g. grounded, trusting, expansive, clear, certain, confident, aligned, free, easeful, in flow, abundant, magnetic, radiant or loving)

— What is fuelling your 'ups' and how you can align to more of this? (e.g. enlisting the help of a coach; asking for support; meditating and journalling; moving through resistance and doing the work anyway; exercising; spending time in nature; taking calming herbal medicines; writing out your fears and clearing them away; spending time away from work with friends and an excellent cheeseboard—with wine, of course)

— What is triggering your 'downs', and how you can learn from this and shift out of it? (e.g. comparing yourself to others; zooming ahead into the future; pushing through fatigue instead of listening to your body; getting stuck in your head and not coming back into your body)

— What gives you the biggest rush of all? Are you honouring enough of this right now? (e.g. letting yourself trust and know that your vision is possible for you; giving yourself space and time to reflect and reset; mapping out what you wish to manifest and call in next, then taking aligned action to start inviting it in; diving deep into your next project; planning a new adventure; decluttering and tidying up to make space, so you can start embodying your ideal way of living and working)

There are things you can do, if you're finding the roller-coaster exhausting but you can't find the 'Stop, get me off this thing!' button. Read on and decide which ones speak to you.

Come back to what lights you up

We can forget why we wanted to be here in the first place. So take some time to reconnect to the vision that you once held so close.

What lights you up about the work you're doing, and the vision you're creating? Why did you want to do this in the first place? Can you reconnect with this? If not ... will you allow yourself to pivot and course-correct?

Step away from your work

No problem can be solved from the same level of consciousness that created it.

Albert Einstein

The constant 'Have I done enough?' can pervade our minds. If we can trust that we have done enough, we can change our world.

Now, you're probably not on your computer right at this moment. However I imagine it's either very close to you, or in some form you're wondering whether if you've done enough today (or this week). So first thing's first: close your laptop (or your mode of work) and back away slowly. (Or run away very fast, preferably straight into a nap/the ocean/a bath/bed/yoga studio/ huge mug of tea.)

Just as you gave yourself permission to trust yourself at the beginning of this book, you have to give yourself permission to know you've done enough. (And especially if you're feeling exhausted from your work. Then you've really done enough for today, and possibly this week.)

When things are feeling exhausting, stagnant or stuck in life and work, taking a step back to allow you to see the bigger picture can really help. I often find that if I give myself a break during a particularly tough moment or day, I feel more energised when I go back to work, and ideas and solutions come through to me during the break as well. (Of course, ideas and solutions don't always come through, but I get to rest and take a break, and that's energising in itself.)

It's often said that our best ideas come to us in the spaces in between. Yet how often do you try to push through a challenge, without giving it (or yourself) space to see a different perspective? The truth is that allowing yourself to see the bigger picture often helps you see that it's not as bad, hard or challenging as you think.

If nothing else, when you look back at how you managed a particular issue, you'll build your resilience (which is a skill in itself) and your trust in your ability to beautifully manage whatever lies ahead.

See it all as an experiment

A few years after I went through a challenging period in my business, I decided to change tactics. Instead of seeing everything I did in my business as serious and high-pressure, I decided to see everything as an experiment.

I dialled the pressure way back, and turned the joy back on. Doing this meant I approached my work more effortlessly, because I wasn't making everything a draining big deal.

Try this for a little while: have fun, take the pressure off, take things less personally, and let yourself enjoy what you're doing in a new way.

Go easy on yourself

In a similar way to seeing things as an experiment, you're allowed to go easy on yourself.

In the past, whenever I've found the ride to feeling aligned and unstoppable a little trying, it's usually because I've either:
— set incredibly high expectations of myself or my work;
— been incredibly tough on myself;
— not acknowledged how far I've come; or
— spent too much energy looking outside my own business or life path, comparing it to others.

It's easy—and important—to set goals in business and life. But it's also common to not reach every single goal you've set for yourself.

It came as a shock to me, when I first realised I wasn't a failure if I didn't hit (and exceed) every target I set for myself. I now accept that it's okay to set a goal and not reach it. It's okay to not be exactly where you thought you 'should' be. It doesn't mean you've failed, or that you haven't tried hard enough, or that you've done something wrong.

So if you're not where you think you should be, can you allow yourself to be exactly where you are right now? It's from this space and energy that you'll find the insight to guide your next decisions and actions—the decisions and actions that'll move you further towards your dreams, or something better.

Love your disappointments

I was sitting at my desk working on a project, when my phone rang. A collaboration I'd been hoping for with a wonderful business had just fallen through. With a smile on my face, I thanked the voice on the other end, hung up, and promptly burst into tears.

I called my husband. I texted a couple of girlfriends. And then I put on Ellie Goulding's *Anything Could Happen* as loudly as my laptop would allow. I made tea. I opened a packet of organic oatmeal raisin cookies I'd just bought that morning (so prepared!). And I got back to work.

Moral of the story: *Always have a fresh box of cookies ready to open when disappointment strikes.*

No wait, that's not right. Do the work, show up, hold your vision in your sights and energy, set goals and work towards your dreams. Let yourself think big, and big, and bigger. (And when needed, start small.) And then, if it doesn't all go to your plan? Trust the bigger one.

Take a deep breath. Eat a cookie (optional, but highly recommended). Pump the music. Then do it all over again, course-correcting, pivoting and changing your mindset and energy, as and when needed (or nudged).

Assess what's making you feel stuck

Every time I've found myself back on the roller-coaster, it's because something is feeling stuck in my business, creativity or life. It could be that I'm fixating on a specific goal or outcome; that I'm not allowing myself time to restore my energy before moving onto the next project or task; that I'm complicating things; that I'm feeling stuck in a kind of self-loathing particular to creatives and writers; or making a part of myself believe I need to do more, in order to be worthy of the flow that's always in our reach.

What's making you feel stuck right now? You might want to grab your journal or a notebook and allow your hand to form the words for you. (Don't overthink what you write. This is the perfect chance to practise trusting and listening to your Higher Self.)

Questions you might like to answer:
— What's making you feel stuck?
— What are you trying to control?
— What would invite flow back in?
— What do you need to let go of to step into flow?
— What do you need to embody to step into flow?
— Will you give yourself permission to do all of this?
— Is there anything else you need to do, say, or allow for yourself?

Keep following the nudges

In a repeat of what's happened to me before, the idea for this book came through while I was still writing, editing, and then launching my second book (the idea for that book came through before my first book had even launched).

It was the week before my book launch tour for *It's All Good* and I'd sent an email to my publisher saying, 'So ... I know the timing of this is hilarious, but here's my idea for book three. Are you keen?'

I still didn't know exactly what this third book would look like, but I knew the key themes: energy, emotions, self-belief, creativity and more, all tied together with a deep drive and devotion to honouring your dreams. But still, I didn't know what it would look like; I simply knew I had to write it.

At times, I'd say to myself and my Guides, 'Maybe I'm not meant to write this book. How can I write this book? I think someone else should. In fact, they've probably already written it.' The reply from my Guides was constant, gentle encouragement; so after a while I stopped second-guessing myself, got a coffee and put fingers to keyboard.

The main reason I was both sure and unsure about writing this book was because, in truth, it was a call for me step up and play bigger in my life, work and business. I was pregnant for much of the writing process (Asher, my baby girl, is now seven months old and currently strapped to me, sleeping while I edit), so it was also a call to surrender to the flow of creativity, to what my energy was doing each day, and to the bigger picture and timing at play. I could not force this book, just like we can't force our dreams.

Writing this book called for me to live, and own, my message, as we're so often called to do when embodying our soul gifts, doing the work we love the most, and speaking up.

I always find that the Universe sends little hints our way, then bigger and bigger hints, when we're really needing to hear a message. In the months leading up to starting the writing process, I kept bumping into people—old family friends, old schoolfriends—who'd ask me how my nutrition business was going. Ha! Remember, I hadn't worked solely as a nutritionist in almost seven years, and the fact that there were people who still thought of me as a nutritionist sometimes irked me.

But by feeling triggered, I was nudged to speak up more. So I'd answer with, 'Oh, I haven't worked as a nutritionist for years.

I'm an author, kinesiologist and business alignment coach now, with some naturopathy on the side.'

When you keep following the nudges, you'll see that you're being guided in how and what to create, every step of the way. The evidence will start to pile up in your favour. Every part of you will exhale, feeling more optimistic and more on purpose, than if you were to continue thinking that you're doing it all by yourself.

Refocus on the energy of your creations

When we put too much focus on the externals—the likes, the comments, the external success, the praise from others, the goals we want to hit—we pull focus away from our source. Our source of energy, of creativity, of trust, of self-confidence. Then we can forget why we're doing this in the first place.

To come back into alignment with what we're creating, and with where we are on this journey, we must refocus, and tune into the energy of what we're creating again. We must let ourselves envision, ground into and step onto the path we're carving for ourselves—the one that deepens our passions, purpose and soul-based gifts.

This means tuning back into source, into the core reasons for why we're wanting to show up in this way: to acknowledge our desire to create something outside of ourselves, and to fulfil the burning need that asks us to empty ourselves of our best work.

This doesn't mean you need to be clear on your bigger purpose all the time. There are times when it feels like we have no idea what we're working on (or working towards), and that's okay. But you can tune into the energy of your business again, the energy of your creativity, the energy of your vessel of choice to expand your work—and your impact—in this world.

When we're too tuned into the ups and downs of the external world, we can sometimes forget to come back to what'll support us as we work towards our dreams—connecting back in with ourselves—so that when the waves of purposeful living rock us back and forth, we stay steady (and confident, and trusting) within ourselves.

Stay in your lane
It's natural to want to be successful, to have recognition and visibility, and to feel supported from your work and on your path. But if we're feeling a little low, it can seem as if everyone around us has it right, and we've missed the boat somehow.

(Side note: In high school, I had a lovely friend who often didn't understand jokes. Once, after another friend had cracked a joke and my friend hadn't understood it, someone said to her, 'Oh, you've missed the boat.' With a curious look on her face, my friend replied, 'What boat?' I still laugh about it to this day.)

That's how we can feel sometimes, doing our work, running our own business or working towards what we truly desire when things aren't feeling clear—like we've missed the boat. It can seem as though we're the only ones who don't have the secret sauce, the formula that seems to work. On those days, we just aren't sure if we'll get to the place we're dreaming about.

This is when you must decide that you know you are enough— no-one else can do that for you. This is when you must allow yourself to close off from outer distractions and cultivate an inner peace by staying in your own lane; by acknowledging that the grass is greener where you pay it the most attention, where you water it and give it light and shade and fertilise it and prune it; where you show it love and let it grow of its own accord.

And you'll do that by releasing comparison, trusting that there's space for you too, and honouring every step (and trip) on your path along the way to purposeful, soul-based living and creating.

It's natural to experience ebbs and flows in life and work

And finally ... accept that life and work aren't always smooth sailing. However, the 'downs' of business don't have to be the pits. They don't have to define you; in fact, they can fuel you. The 'ups' don't have to define you either; they can fuel you too.

An essence for alignment

Gentian is a great Bach flower essence to use here. It'll support you in clearing away any disappointment you may feel when experiencing setbacks in your life or work. It'll re-energise you, encouraging you to keep going.

ALIGNED AND UNSTOPPABLE AFFIRMATIONS

— *I trust in the bigger plan and the greater vision for my work, path and purpose.*
— *I stand true and solid in the energy of what I'm creating.*
— *I allow ease into my life and work.*
— *I allow myself to reach my goals and intentions easily.*
— *I flow with wherever I am.*

CHAPTER 19

Confidence, Love and Flow

I was working with a client, Zoe, who was feeling really stressed about money. She'd been working in her coaching business for several years, and had dealt with a lot of sticky, old, negative feelings, perceptions and self-sabotages around herself and the 'enoughness' of her work. While she thought she'd dealt with this, it was resurfacing again, as she embarked on a new way of working in her business.

As well as feeling stressed about money, Zoe had been going through a period of comparing herself to her industry peers, especially people who'd she deemed 'had it easy', who seemed to always have everything (launching programs, bringing in money, receiving clients and media mentions) down so easily.

(Of course, this was Zoe's perception, and the story she was telling herself. It's very likely her industry peers were also working their activewear-clad butts off, just like she was.)

Zoe was worried about all kinds of bills, including an upcoming tax bill, and how she'd bring in enough new clients to pay for these bills, as well as her regular living and business expenses. She said to me, 'Strangely enough, I don't feel like I'm doubting my abilities, but I know I'm doubting myself, if that makes sense ... doubting that I can bring in more money easily, doubting that I'll know what to do next, and that it'll be a good decision for me. I'm just feeling really stuck. I know what I want to work towards, but it feels like nothing is happening!'

Zoe admitted that she thought this period in her business would be easier, or at least there'd be more movement and momentum, because of how excited she was feeling about her work and how hard she'd been working, but that she also felt a bit stuck as to how to express and communicate her work. She said, 'I already feel like I'm blocking people, even though I know my work is so helpful.'

While she had confidence in her coaching, there was also an underlying fear of, 'Ugh, why would they bother? There are better people, programs and prices to choose from. There are too many obstacles, why choose me?'

Zoe felt like she didn't know how to proceed (her feeling of 'stuckness'). Yet she also knew that to move forwards meant to take action in a way that felt easy and aligned; to stay open and excited about her work; and most importantly, to be herself. She trusted her work and her offerings; now she had to trust and back herself.

She said it always felt like there was a block in relation to the growth of her business. When I asked her why she felt that, she said she wasn't sure, even though she knew she was good enough. 'Oh,' she said, 'perhaps my perfectionism is flaring up.' We laughed, took sips of our tea, then got down to business.

We did some coaching and energetic clearing work around releasing her two specific fears and worries. The first was fear of coming across as 'too coachy'—she didn't want to be perceived as a pushy coach, a cookie-cutter coach, or a 'hustle to burnout' coach. I assured her that this would never happen, if she stayed in alignment with herself and her dreams and goals. 'How can you promote a way of living and working, if you don't live or work like that yourself?' I asked her.

Her second worry was a (perceived) negative thought that it was easier for everyone else. This made her feel she'd never be able to experience ease in her business. Her false idea that other people have some 'secret sauce' to success was holding her back, keeping her stuck in a cycle of victimhood and negative thoughts.

Zoe would look at people who'd done it before and see the external ease they portrayed. But of course, she had very little insight into the hours of work, love, sweat and tears they had put into their work. She also couldn't see how others perceived her; others may well have been thinking that Zoe had what they were working towards. While stuck in this pattern of thinking, she wasn't looking at what she'd already created, achieved and accomplished in her own life and business.

To clear this, and to stay in her own lane, she had to do a few things:

— Come back to herself, and trust her work and her own path.
— Allow things to be easy for herself too, without comparing herself to other people, or making up stories about how 'easy' or 'hard' their life or business was in relation to hers. She had to clear the fear of allowing things to be easy in her business and life.
— Clear away the old stories, fears, negative beliefs and contraction she was feeling, and open into ease, flow, alignment and abundance.

Here are the goals we aligned Zoe to:

— I allow myself to bring in more money, more easily.

— I am allowed to work less hours, and earn more money.

— I am allowed to uplevel my business, my mindset and my thoughts, in order to receive more.

— I am always abundantly financially supported.

— I can easily and generously support myself and my family.

— I love money and receive and hold it with an open heart and open arms.

— I allow myself to be financially successful and supported, by allowing myself to receive more.

— I recognise how far I've come and I'm grateful for everything I've already created.

— I allow myself to step up into the next level of my life and work.

— I allow myself to receive with ease.

What came up first were two blocks in her chakras. The first was in her Crown chakra, which relates to feeling guided and supported by a higher power, as well as trusting in abundance. When I asked her to tap into what that meant for her, she said it was about listening to guidance, and knowing she was supported. Deep down, she knew she was being looked after—she knew more clients were always on their way, and that she could always receive more money. She got the message: *Keep going now, to create and receive more ease later.*

The second block came up around her Third Eye chakra, which relates to intuition, foresight, clarity and bigger vision. The message was simple: *Keep doing this work now, and you'll receive; this is all in line with your bigger vision.* This was about her staying on her path towards her bigger vision and what she envisioned for her life and business. She knew this stage was important for the foundations of her future, and that the only way ahead was to keep moving forwards.

I pulled three cards for her, and they related to communication (inviting her to continue to speak up for desired results in her business), rest (to prepare for what she was about to receive), and her Base chakra (building a strong foundation by consciously creating).

The message for Zoe in a nutshell: keeping up communication and speaking up about her message and her work; resting and restoring her energy; and continuing to create, to further develop her base. What a great plan.

We added in one more goal:

— I consciously create my desired outcome (or something better) and allow myself to receive this with love, ease and gratitude.

Then an essence came up, in relation to her kinesiology balance: the Australian bush flower essence, Kapok Bush. The energy of this essence is all about responding to life's challenges with perseverance and commitment, by taking control of your life and applying yourself.

Energetically, it relates to the Solar Plexus chakra (supporting your confidence and personal power); the Heart chakra (allowing you to give and receive love—in relation to this balance, we can also see this as giving and receiving money); and the Water element (which relates to allowing yourself to flow, and releasing fear and anxiety).

All of this awareness helped Zoe to clear the sense of stuckness she felt, and create a stronger foundation on which to grow and expand her business. And altogether, this balance was deeply comforting. It was the epitome of becoming aligned and unstoppable: it helped Zoe to become aligned and unstoppable in what she was creating, while allowing her to receive along the way.

You can do it

You will be the one who creates your reality, consciously. So take the time you need to gather any unhelpful, low-vibrational, energy-sucking thoughts that are holding you back from expanding, from taking action, and from knowing your worth.

You will be the one who can do this for yourself. You will be the one to discard those old thoughts, decide on your new ones, and take action on them.

You won't always know how things will work out, but you'll know you're capable of creating, of honouring your gifts, and of showing up. And that's what matters.

Take some time to do this now. Write down some of the old, negative, fearful thoughts that are currently swirling through your mind and energy. (I know you've done this in an earlier chapter, but this is how you build a practice of knowing yourself, clearing away fears, and taking aligned action.) I find putting them down on paper gives them a place to live that doesn't use your oxygen, or your life force.

Thank those thoughts—they truly think they're keeping you safe. But where you are right now is safe, and where you want to go will be safe too ... because you are what is safe. So thank the old thoughts, and welcome in the new.

What are the new, uplifting, positive, confident thoughts you wish to embody and align to, that'll help you move towards what you're creating? Focus on those. The other thoughts might linger, and that's okay. They might come back, and that's okay. They might morph into different fears or thoughts, and that's okay too.

If there's one thing I remember from Year 9 science, it's that energy can't be destroyed—it can only change form. Our goal isn't to destroy negative thoughts, but to transmute and transform their energy into something positive, powerful and uplifting.

The point is not to banish your fear, but to feed your courage. This is where your victory, your confidence, and your focus lives and breathes. This is how you become aligned and unstoppable.

JOURNALLING PROMPT

How might your day play out, if you were focused on powerful, positive and uplifting thoughts (instead of listening to your inner critic/negative thoughts)?

ALIGNED AND UNSTOPPABLE AFFIRMATION

*I easily create positive, powerful and uplifting thoughts
that transmute and transform all that no longer serves
me, feeding my courage, strengthening my confidence and
supporting me in becoming aligned and unstoppable.*

CHAPTER 20

This Beautiful Cycle

There'll be a time (or many) when you ask yourself if you're doing enough. You'll wonder if you're on the right track; if someone else in your position—exactly in your position—would be further ahead of you right now. What might've happened if you'd said 'yes' to that one opportunity; if you'd done one more push to get on that hot new podcast as a guest; if you'd gone left instead of right; if you had/hadn't gone to that networking event ... if, if, if.

When this kind of thinking pops up, it's our shadow self wondering if we are enough. And your deepest self knows that you always are.

I don't say this to dust lightly over your fears; but I do believe that most of us are always trying our best. Sometimes our best doesn't get us to what our minds, goals or hearts were set on, but our best is enough. You know why? Because you're doing all you can with what you have and what you know, right now. If you constantly wonder if you're enough, and then tell yourself that even your best isn't enough, how will you ever step ahead, towards the life you wish to create?

If you constantly tell yourself you're not doing enough—if you never, ever believe that your best is enough—then even your 'perfect' best won't be enough. Even the work you idealise in yourself, the part of your future self that you've put on a pedestal, that won't even be enough. And you'll never get to fully see, enjoy or take part in what your future self creates, if you can't appreciate what you've already done, or how far you've already come.

Not all of your dreams will come true, but the ones that count will.

If you could've done better, you would have. But you started where you were, with what you had. Next time—because you will give yourself that chance, right?—you'll know more. Maybe you'll do it differently, or better. And that'll be enough. And then next time, you'll know even more. Maybe you'll do it differently, or better. And that'll be enough.

Do you see? Do you see this beautiful cycle? You made it. Do you see how it begins? With starting, making, showing up, and trusting yourself, your creativity, your voice, your vision and your enoughness.

Your work is enough; it's enough. It's always deepening and ever-changing. And so are you.

Your work is enough

There's a saying: *A rising tide lifts all boats.*

I started my business in 2011, but I only started blogging in early 2012. That was when I realised there was an entire online world ... and I felt like a very small fish in a very large pond.

I went through a stage where I compared myself to every other blogger, health coach and naturopath out there. It was painful—my inner critic was raging at me, telling me I wasn't good enough, that I'd never have what someone else had, that all the good ideas were taken.

I remember how I felt when I landed on someone else's website, with all these nasty thoughts swirling through my mind. I remember how small I would feel when someone shared their success online, and I felt like there wasn't any space for me to be successful too.

I remember thinking—as so many of us often do—that it was always so much easier for other people. I made up (and listened to) countless deeply embedded excuses (that often morphed into blocks) as to why I couldn't create what I saw in others.

Sometimes the guilt I felt for feeling envious made me feel even more envious. I would think, *They're probably never jealous or comparing themselves to others, I'm crazy!*

But in truth, I don't know anyone who hasn't compared themselves to someone else. Especially when you're working towards something big and bold in your life; especially when you're seeing other people creating what—on some level—you desire too.

It can be so painful, and most of the time, it doesn't just go away by itself. It takes love, compassion, forgiveness, awareness and courage. It takes daily practice, until it becomes your new way of being. It will keep coming up for you until you realise this truth: *What I see in you, I see in me too.*

When I would see someone else's shiny new offering or opportunity and feel a twinge of envy and the drag of comparison, it was only because I knew deep down that I could—and wanted to—create something that beautiful too. This realisation hit me after months of continuous comparisonitis.

And so I finally decided to rise. I decided I was tired of my inner critic pushing and pulling me down. I realised that our envy or jealousy is simply a beacon, guiding us in the right direction, reflecting a part of ourselves back to us.

If it's calling to you, you must listen to it. It's asking you to become clear on what you want, and to make a choice and a commitment to yourself about your dreams and your goals. And to then step up, take action, align yourself in the direction you want to head and shine your light to help you get there.

So, listen to your comparison. Listen to your envy. Make friends with it. Dig deeper into why a specific person triggers you, and what they trigger in you. Is it a desire to be seen? To show up? To create more?

Let your envy fuel your success. If you don't listen to your envy in the right way, it'll take a hold of you and prevent you from rising.

Envy vibrates at a low vibration, until you rise above it. You have the power to release yourself from those emotions and move forwards. But only you have that power.

Remove obstacles yourself

In a yoga class, my teacher once explained how she used to be guided by Ganesha, the Hindi elephant god of wisdom and learning, and how she used to think Ganesha would help her remove obstacles in her life ... until she just kept getting blocked by them. Then she realised she was just being shown the obstacles, but she had to remove them herself.

Your envy, jealousy, sense of lack or 'competition' is a block, an obstacle, something that'll keep you stuck—if you don't clear and release the block. While it may be helpful in showing you what's possible for you, it's also keeping you stuck exactly where you are, if you do nothing about it.

It's completely draining to deny yourself your dreams. By not taking action when you're stuck in comparison, you're continuing to drain your own energy.

So you must take action. The 'action' can be as simple as a quick journalling session, or as profound as deep healing and forgiveness; letting go of procrastination and taking one action to move you forwards; calling your energy and power back through your intention; looking within, instead of 'without'; combining fate and freewill to trust that you're supported while you take your next steps; and trusting that what is meant for you will not pass you by.

That quiet, insidious panic—the deep sense that you're not enough, or that you've done something wrong, or that everyone knows something you don't—that you might be feeling, could come from a realisation that you've wedged yourself in a comparison trap of your own creation.

That's not just the part of you seeking comfort and compassion from within. It's also the deep part of you who knows you're worthy of success—the part that wants to go forth and take action. That's also the part ready to help release yourself from the trap. After all, you created the trap; so you have the key/map/plan to escape it too.

So be compassionate to yourself. Look at what you've already done. Let your envy and comparison guide you to take action. Let it shift you in the direction of your dreams, let it move you forwards, then work towards and receive what you know you can create (or something better) in your own way, all in good time.

Make up your mind(set)

You can also part ways with envy and comparison by creating an abundant mindset, and knowing there's enough for you.

A little while ago, a long time after I'd decided to rise above the relentless chitter-chatter of my envious inner critic, I received an email from a fellow biz owner announcing her latest launch. For a moment, I felt triggered into lack again. *I want what she has*, I thought.

Then I realised that's exactly what the triggering emotion was reminding me to do: step up, decide to rise, align to what I want, and know there's enough space for me.

So, I sent her some love and a quick email: *I love what you're doing. It looks gorgeous! Sending you so much love. I hope it's all going so well for you. Cass x.*

Beaming love to the person you're comparing yourself to will help lift you both up. (Even if they don't know you've sent them love, you'll know; and it'll change the dynamics within yourself.)

If you're feeling like you're caught in a trap of your own making, extending love to someone else is a way to open the doors for you to receive too. It's a mirror—if you wish to receive, you must give too. A rising tide lifts all boats, remember?

So, know there's enough space for you too. Know there's enough time for you to do it. Know there are enough resources for you to create it. Know there's enough knowledge and passion and purpose inside you, to make your dreams come true.

When you feel triggered by someone or something, you don't need to shrink back, or feel smaller, scared or unworthy. Because you are worthy too.

Once I realised that, in reality, I was the only person able to give myself permission to stop comparing myself to others (or at least to have the awareness I needed to help me move closer to my dreams), then I realised I had some (inner) work to do. Instead of trying to suppress what I was feeling, or blindly talk myself out of it, I sat with how I was feeling. I brought my attention and energy back to myself, within.

If we're constantly looking outside of ourselves, we're looking 'without', and that word has two meanings here. Firstly, we're looking externally to ourselves and seeking validation and affirmation from elsewhere. Secondly, we're looking at everything 'without'—from a space of lack and competition.

When we're in that space, we focus on what we don't have. We focus on where we aren't. We focus on 'the other'. When we do that, we make up stories:

> It's so much easier for her. He knows what he's doing, and I don't. If only she knew what it was like for me. He has help that I don't have. She knows something I don't know. He is braver. She is smarter. He is more ambitious. She is more popular.

We make up excuses about why we don't have what we want, and why we probably never will. We decide that everyone else knows something we don't, that they had help, that they had more connections, knew more people, were in the right place at the right time. They were 'lucky', and we were not.

There's a little bit of magic and synchronicity involved in all stories of success and achievement. But mostly, it comes down to your mindset and your actions; to the inner work you do, and the way this reflects the outer work you do. To the way you show up, step up, and step out. And that is up to you.

Make up your mind(set). Before you berate yourself for comparing, how can you be compassionate? How can you see that your envy is, in fact, guiding you? How can you send the apple of your (comparison) eye some love, then gather up your energy, call it back to you, ground into the present moment, and trust yourself and exactly where you are right now?

Okay, and then what?

Once you start to release negative, limiting beliefs, and start to consciously work to uplevel your thoughts to believe that you are worthy, this is what can and will start to happen:

— You can start to feel really excited by the prospect of growing your business, moving forwards in your career, getting back into work if you've taken some time out, or simply stepping up into what's next for you in your life, without focusing on what everyone else is doing.

— You'll no longer feel stressed or anxious when you see someone else doing something that you know you'd love to do too. And if that old feeling creeps back in, you'll trust that you can let yourself feel it, then clear it out with compassion and action.

— You'll feel yourself softening, allowing yourself to become more patient. No longer will you feel the pressures of time, or that you can't create/do something new because time is running out.

— You'll start to feel more supported in the work you do, and in how you create it.

— You'll stop feeling so overwhelmed, because you'll trust the timing of your own life.

— You'll feel more energised by your work and purpose, and more powerful because of it.

Oh, and if you do find yourself feeling caught in perfectionism, or feeling impatient, stressed, over-worked, worried, overwhelmed, out-of-sorts, vulnerable, stuck in lack, scared to move forwards, comparing yourself to others, or experiencing any other 'symptom' of trying to do your best work so that you can show up as the best version of yourself (for yourselves and those you love) then guess what? You'll also know you're human, and what you're feeling is more than okay, and you won't punish yourself for it.

You'll do the forgiveness work, you'll send yourself love and compassion, you'll give yourself a break.

You'll know one uncomfortable or stressful moment, hour or day does not undo all the work you're doing.

You'll know you are worthy of creating and receiving what you want in business and life, whether you're starting up at home after having a baby, in corporate, in a small boutique business, planning your next move, or running your own biz on the oceans of wherever you find yourself.

If you stay focused on yourself, on your own body of work and on your own path, you'll see your dreams come true (in their own way).

Next time you find yourself smothered in self-doubt, remind yourself that your viewpoint of your life and work is important, valid and unique; that you have everything you need right now; that you're exactly where you need to be right now, in order to move forwards to where you're envisioning.

If that doesn't help, my favourite thing to do is back away from my work. Sometimes when we worry our work isn't good enough, it's being triggered by fatigue. That is especially true if we've been pushing ourselves too hard, for too long, in an attempt to prove to ourselves (or to someone else) that we are indeed worthy.

My mum always says everything feels worse when you're tired—and aren't mums always right?

When you give yourself a little brain holiday, you can come back to your work refocused and refreshed. You can find your voice again—that voice that helps you write, create, share, visualise, show up, dream and feel grounded in your perception of the world.

ALIGNED AND UNSTOPPABLE AFFIRMATION

I am enough, my work is enough, and I'm exactly where I'm supposed to be.

CHAPTER 21

Jump When You're Ready

We're often told to 'just leap', right? To just do it and get stuck into it. And while I'm a huge proponent of starting before you're ready (as you know, it's how I started my business, just a month after graduating), I also believe there are times when it's best to listen to the part of you that knows you're not ready yet ... but that you will be, soon, and to trust the timing of that knowledge.

I grew up horseriding and went through a stage, when I was about 13 or 14 years old, when I became really fearful of showjumping. I wasn't even jumping very high jumps at the time, but I just wasn't interested in pushing through my fear.

I can't remember why I became scared in the first place (perhaps I fell off during a showjumping round) but whatever the reason, there was a period of many months when I simply didn't want to jump. It terrified me.

My friends would go off jumping, and I'd stick to my routine (on very flat, safe ground) with Melody, my beautiful liver chestnut pony. Every so often, my instructor and friends would try to coax me back into the ring with promises that I could start small, that

Melody could easily jump that height, that I'd done it before so I could do it again. But nope, I wasn't doing it.

At times I wondered if I'd ever jump again. My friends and I had planned our futures, with dreams of all of us riding in the Olympics, then owning and running a farm and training horses together. We decided I'd be in charge of the dressage training, since I clearly wasn't going to be training the showjumping horses!

Then one day, seemingly out of the blue (but really, a culmination of all the days that had come and gone), I felt braver than before. I joined my friends and their horses in the showjumping ring. I told my instructor I was ready. And I jumped.

Afterwards, when Melody and I were back on solid ground, when I realised I was safe and that I could do it, and that it had been the right time for me to jump, I realised I'd been afraid of fear itself—I had made it all so much worse in my head. For months, I'd talked myself out of something that I knew I could do; something that I wanted to do, when the time was right for me. (Not to mention that of course, my pony could obviously do it; I had quite literally been ignoring the support carrying me forwards.)

Doing it once gave me confidence; the jumping was magical, and I was ready to do it again. I became ready to do it in my own time. The fact that I'd spent months telling myself I wasn't ready didn't matter anymore.

Years later came Commander Joe, a wise liver chestnut horse (and old-school showjumping champion) who taught me not just how to jump, but how to fly. As I won blue ribbon after blue ribbon in showjumping competitions, I realised that because I'd taken my own sweet time to get there, I was enjoying it even more.

(As an aside: at showjumping competitions, as I'd walk him around the grounds, people would come up to me and ask me if he was Commander Joe. 'Yes!' My grin—and my pride—was huge. He'd been a champion for so many years, he was practically famous. He passed away quite suddenly, when I was 15; he'd been 25 and still jumping just days before. That is almost unheard of, for a horse his age. I gathered as many names and addresses of his past owners as I could, wrote them all letters and included recent photos of him, then posted them off, tears in my eyes. I still cry every time I think about him. Yes, crying right now.)

Those blue ribbons meant more to me, because I knew I'd deeply earned them, and for all the right reasons. Sweet Melody taught me how to face my fears, and beautiful Joe taught me how to honour and appreciate every step of the journey. Then came handsome Johnny Walker (yes, spelled differently to the whiskey), who I got to train, thanks to years of confidence gained from Melody and Joe. (We won't talk about Foaly, the little grey pony who bucked me off—into the mud—every chance she got; or Jesse, the gorgeous dun, who was like the seriously handsome bad boy that every girl wants to tame ... but can't!)

On reflection, I realised that my period of not jumping was readying me to jump, in my own time, and in my own way. I realised you don't need to be an overnight success to be a success, on your own terms, and in your own time. (In actual fact, you're only an overnight success to those who've just discovered you. To you, you might be a decades-long success story.)

Your dreams might take time, and they'll definitely take grit, determination, a fierce focus and a deep devotion. And that's perfect, because there's no rush. You can jump when you're ready. And by jumping when you're ready, you allow yourself to expand into what's next for you at the right time for you, without feeling as though you're rushing, racing or trying to do things for the sake of it, or worse, for other people.

There will definitely be times in your life when clearing fears and moving through resistance is the way to go; but on the flip side, it's important you honour the times when you simply need more time.

JOURNALLING PROMPT

What can you do (or say to yourself) to stay aligned and inspired while you get ready to 'jump'?

ALIGNED AND UNSTOPPABLE AFFIRMATION

I allow myself to take time to build my dreams and solidly create my path ahead. I'm always exactly where I'm supposed to be.

CHAPTER 22

Expand Up, Out and Beyond

On our way to achieving our dreams, we'll be called to go back to basics, to expand up and out and beyond, and to do things that terrify us, all in the name of expansion.

When I started practising as a naturopath, I had this amazing mentor. Anytime I'd go to her feeling overwhelmed about how to treat a client, she would say to me, 'Just give them passionflower!' This was her way of saying, 'Just go simple. Don't overthink it.'

By first giving clients passionflower, a beautifully calming herb, you'd help them move out of the stress response, into a more relaxed state. When people feel calmer, more grounded and relaxed, you can support them even more deeply.

'Just give them passionflower!' became my mantra. I applied it to all sorts of situations, whenever I felt overwhelmed. Of course, it didn't mean I always gave my clients passionflower to start with, but it did mean I always let myself go back to basics and start small, to help my clients in the way that best supported them.

Stretched and pulled

I remember a time a potential new client got in touch with me for business alignment coaching. This person was—according to the story I made up in my head—more successful than I was at the time. I checked out their website and social media, and then started to feel really worried about how I would help them.

How could I help someone who might be way 'beyond' where I currently was? Wouldn't they already know more than I did, be more confident than I was, and have more skills and experience?

Then I realised that working with clients who you deem are more successful than you are is a way of deepening your work, because you must rise to the occasion; you must expand up, out and beyond what you thought was possible. You must leave your ego at the door. You must remember this is about resonance, not numbers. It's about expansion, not maths. It's about being confident enough within to trust yourself, your work, your path and your guidance; trusting the right clients and opportunities are flowing to you, because you're in alignment, and because you're able to receive them.

It's about knowing that you might be stretched and pulled on the path to ascension and expansion, and knowing you wouldn't have it any other way.

For you to grow in alignment, you must also see where you want to be. And sometimes this means stretching before you think you're ready.

You can handle it

In a similar way, you might sometimes be given experiences that show you what you're capable of, even if they terrify you.

When I was nearing the end of my kinesiology studies, we had to do six months of student clinic. Anyone from the general public could book in to see us. We'd go into the clinic room in pairs, so there was always one student practitioner and one student observer. Our teacher would pop into each clinic room during the session to observe, for just a few moments, then move on to the next room.

At the beginning of the clinic session, I put my hand up first (as usual). So off I went to see my very first kinesiology client, accompanied by Matt, one of my student peers.

I walked into the clinic room and handed my client (Melanie, a girl in her late teens) a clipboard with a form to fill out. Something felt a little bit off. Melanie wouldn't make eye contact and seemed to be muttering to herself. Her mum, who'd come along with her, took the clipboard from her and filled out the form.

When she was finished, I scanned the form. My client had schizophrenia. 'Okay,' I thought, 'I have no experience with this, but I'll go slowly, easily and gently.'

There was one good reason I continued on with this session, instead of leaving the room to speak to my supervisor and say I didn't think this client should be in a student clinic. Matt, the student accompanying me for the session, was a clinical psychiatrist with about 30 years' experience. Phew!

I said a silent prayer of thanks to the Universe that I'd been paired with Matt for this session. I looked him straight in the eye, my apprehension clearly evident, and he gave me an imperceptible nod. I was good to go, and he had my back.

So I took a deep breath, prepared my notes and folders, and started the session. It soon became clear that Melanie was not doing well. (Matt later told me he believed she was actually having a psychotic break during the session.) It was quite scary for me, and I was completely out of my comfort zone.

When the session ended, I asked to speak to my client's mum outside the room. Since she hadn't written much about her daughter's medical care on the form, I double-checked whether her daughter was on medication, and whether she had a doctor or psychiatrist she could see in the next few days. The answer was 'no' and 'no'. Melanie's mum said it was too expensive to look after her daughter, and that's why she thought it would be good to come to this student clinic. I called Matt in to speak to the mum. He gave her some sound advice on what she needed to do next, to get her daughter the care she desperately needed.

I was furious, scared and shaken. As soon as Melanie and her mum had left the clinic, I closed the door and fell on the floor in a heap, sobbing in fright and relief. I couldn't believe what had just happened.

I couldn't believe there hadn't been some level of screening beforehand. I didn't want to judge, but I also couldn't believe the mother wasn't seeking appropriate care for her daughter, when the free healthcare system in Australia is so amazing. I couldn't believe my luck that Matt had been in the room with me the whole time. I couldn't believe I'd managed the session. I couldn't believe any of it.

Matt came and knelt down by my crouched, shaking body, tilting his head to one side to look me in the eye. He seemed surprised to see me completely losing it. 'You did so well!' he said. 'I didn't know you were feeling worried during the session. You kept it together so well, you did such a good job.' With his support, I calmed down; I quite literally picked myself up and dusted myself off. I took a deep breath, composed myself, and we went back into the main classroom together, where I told my teacher and peers what had happened.

So ... that was my first kinesiology client!

After that experience, I was imbued with the confidence and knowledge that I was ready to see any kind of client. It was one of the most intense experiences I've ever gone through in relation to my work, but afterwards I knew I could do anything.

You'll always be given what you can manage. Even if it means you go for the simple route. ('Just give them passionflower!') Even if it means you must rise to the occasion—and expand up, out and beyond. Even if it means you fall into a sobbing heap at the end.

ALIGNED AND UNSTOPPABLE AFFIRMATION

*I allow myself to rise into my expansion,
expanding up, out and beyond.*

CHAPTER 23

So ... Am I There Yet?

The biggest break is the one you will give yourself by
choosing to believe in your vision, in what you love, and
in the gifts you have to offer the waiting world.

LESLIE ODOM JR., *FAILING UP*

Have you ever wished that one day you'd wake up and get a phone call that would change everything? Or meet someone who'd take your business to the next level? Or tell you that your work is unique and deeply needed, and they're going to take you so far?

We see it in the movies (and probably feel like we're seeing it on social media) all the time: the struggling artist who gets found and makes it big.

I know that feeling—of wanting to be picked—and I know the remedy for wishing someone would swoop in and make your dreams come true.

The remedy is to know that you need to pick yourself, every single day, in order for someone else to believe in you. It's to believe that you are already your wildest dream because you believe in yourself; it's to know you're the one who can make your dreams (or something better) come true. You're the one who can change everything, who can take your work to the next level, who can believe that your work is unique and deeply needed, and who can deepen your purpose. You're the only one who can take you so far.

You don't need the social media version of Prince Charming to make your work worthwhile, or for someone famous to pick you out of the audience and bring you onto their stage. You don't need validation from people with big Instagram accounts to know your work is valid, valuable and enough. You don't need an invitation to speak in front of a huge crowd to know you have gifts to share.

Of course, it's important to cultivate friendships, contacts and collaborators while you build your dreams from the ground up; but you also need to start counting on yourself. Stop waiting for someone else to come in and change things. Change them yourself.

When you count on yourself, you create the opportunities you are craving to be a part of. You take the action, you make the plans, you put yourself out there. You do the work. You don't wait for the green light from someone else; you're proactive and efficient and you create your own stage on which to stand.

You can't take the old you with you

Sometimes on our way to getting where we want to be, we don't realise that, on some level, we're already there.

One of my clients, Hannah, is incredible at what she does. She's a wife, mum and business owner, and her clients leave her salon feeling like a million bucks. However, like so many of us, she sometimes wonders if she's doing enough to build the life, business and purposeful path she wants.

During one of our sessions together, we were discussing the shifts and changes she'd experienced since our last session. She'd let go of a huge (and very old) limiting belief and story she'd been carrying around that had been placed on her by someone else, and was now feeling ready to move forwards, powerful and free. She said to me: 'To take it to the next level, I have to be at the next level. I can't take the old me with me.'

Hannah was realising that to step up and into the next version of her vision, she had to deepen her belief in herself and in what she was capable of creating and receiving.

So, of course, we energetically aligned her to goals to help her realise—and achieve—this. Her goals centred around following her heart with what she was creating; appreciating and acknowledging how far she'd come; trusting that her work is important, valuable and worthy; feeling confident in her work and proud of what she'd already done; and radiating a deep inner love and self-confidence, supporting her to trust she was exactly where she was supposed to be.

What came up next was for her to clear and release the old, limiting belief and programming of her perception that she wasn't worthy of everything she'd created, and everything she wanted to create. So we added in some more goals:

— I am worthy of what I envision for myself, my family, my business and my life.
— I trust in my ability to attract abundance.
— I open up to the next level of abundance for myself.
— I clear and release any limitations I may be holding onto.
— I trust the next level.
— I focus on my bigger vision.
— I'm worthy of having what I desire, or something even better.
— I focus on the bigger version of what I've already created.

What came up next in her balance was a block in her Throat and Base chakras. When we dug deeper into this, it was a message to her to be really truthful to herself, and then to others, about what she's capable of doing, making and creating in her life.

Seth Godin says: *When in doubt, tell yourself the truth.* This was her truth. Hannah had to stop telling herself she wasn't worthy and instead, tell herself the truth: she could and did believe in herself, and in her ability to step up into the next version of her life and work. She had to pick herself.

She had to acknowledge that what she was doing was already enough, in order to give herself the confidence to continue on. She had to back herself, support herself, and believe in herself. And to do that, she had to start communicating truthfully with herself, clearing and releasing the fears and self-doubts that made her doubt her abilities, and herself.

The leap isn't always a leap

If we're ready to move into what's next for us, we first have to trust the intangible calling that pulls us there. When you want to move to the next stage, you have to be able to recognise and witness the stage you've already created and cultivated for yourself. While you may be tempted, there can be no skipping stages. When the next stage feels far away from where you are, only a leap (and trust and patience) will do.

I've often found that what feels like a leap is sometimes not a leap at all. When we've done the inner work, the leap that feels so huge can actually be the energetic equivalent of one step off a pavement—not terrifying, not huge, but perhaps slightly out of your comfort zone.

When it feels as though you don't know how to move up and into what's next, trust that you can simultaneously accept and acknowledge where you are right now, and be driven to keep moving forwards. Don't let one stop you from doing the other.

As you do so, keep remembering and trusting that it's already enough. Where you are today is already perfect. You can keep building and feel like you've arrived, even if you know there's more for you to create.

This might sound contradictory but what you create in your life is so rarely black and white, right? Let's make space for the greys, the spaces in between the rules we think we need to live by, and relish the freedom and space this creates.

You're 'there' now

I just jumped onto Facebook for a bit of procrastination between chapters (it's been one of those days), and a 'memory' popped up, dated exactly four years ago. It was a status I'd put up, that simply said:

> *If there's a book that you want to read, but it hasn't been written yet, then you must write it.*
>
> Toni Morrison

I wrote that status months before I'd go on to win a book deal to write my first book, the book I'd have wanted to read while stuck in comparison and low self-worth. And it was years before I'd write my second book, the book that I really wanted to read when going through a year of challenges, growth, and uplevelling. So seeing that status appear, when I was writing this book, made me pause.

I paused to give thanks for exactly where I am right now, and to honour that younger version of me, who had no idea what was coming next.

We can set goals and work towards them, but we must acknowledge just how far we've come. We must also acknowledge that, on some level, there's a younger version of ourselves cheering us on, every single day.

When I started my business at 24 years of age, if you'd run me through a grocery list of all the things I'd go on to do in my business over the next several years—all the programs I'd create; the books I'd write; the clients I'd work with; the places I'd travel to; the workshops and seminars I'd run and attend; the events I'd speak at; the people I'd meet; the relationships I'd foster and cherish—I may have said to you, 'Whaaat!!! Really? That list is everything I've dreamed of and more. I can't even imagine all of that happening right now though.' Today's version of me wants to hug the past version of me, and tell her that everything is going to be (more than) okay.

The younger version of you who's cheering you on wants you to know that you're 'there' now (even if you're not exactly where you thought you'd be). There's no more asking, 'Am I there yet?' because there is a constant evolution taking place—of who you are, of what you want, and of what you're calling into your life.

So take that knowledge; keep it close to you, the next time you feel far away from your dreams. Tune into the version of you who wanted what you have now; there'll always be something that comes to mind, even if it feels small and insignificant. Compared to the younger you, you've already made it. You're already there.

I believe that for as long as you know you have work to do, to create, to share, to publish, to launch, to release ... you'll never feel like you're 'there' yet. But you can always be grateful for where you are, while holding the need to continue to create close to you. And that's beautiful.

If one day you believe you have arrived 'there', you may well have emptied yourself of your best work. But from my point of view, being 'here'—where I can create something new every day, continuously emptying myself of my best work—is exactly where I want to be.

JOURNALLING PROMPT

If you 'picked yourself' today—by choosing to fully believe in yourself—what would you do tomorrow?

ALIGNED AND UNSTOPPABLE AFFIRMATION

I trust I'm always exactly where I'm supposed to be,
and able to expand into what's next at the same time.

Part 3

THE CREATIVE WORK

Expression and Creation

CHAPTER 24

A Room of Your Own

*A woman must have money and a room of
her own if she is to write [fiction].*

VIRGINIA WOOLF, *A ROOM OF ONE'S OWN*

This next part is all about the creative side of your work, in all its forms. I'm starting with one of my favourite topics: creating a space, or a room, of your own.

The above quote by the late author, Virginia Woolf, pops into my mind on an almost daily basis. Every time I mention it to my husband he laughs and jokingly says, 'But you don't write fiction!' and I'm like, 'You're missing the point!'

This isn't earth-shattering stuff, but it can make all the difference to how you feel within yourself, when you wish to carve out a space for yourself in the world. I'll admit it: I am an expert at creating a space for myself, whether at home or even on holidays. Perhaps it's the Cancerian in me—the part that loves home and creature comforts. Perhaps it's the organised part of me—the part that loves my space to feel decluttered and comfortable. Perhaps it's something else altogether—the part of me that simply wants to love the surrounds in which I find myself.

Think of the way the Danish live their *hygge* lifestyle (pronounced hoogah); it's all about creating comfort and cosiness. Think mugs of tea, candles, reading nooks, decluttered spaces and a feeling of home. This is what comes to mind when I think about creating a space that feels ripe for creating, for doing the (inner and outer) work, and for carving out your space in the wider world.

The space that you allow yourself to create in, dream in, and vision in will cultivate peace of mind. By creating space for yourself, however you can, you get to create peace of mind, spaciousness and freedom for yourself. From this 'room of your own', you create space to do the work you most want to do.

The space you create will depend on whatever space you have available to you right now. While it might be a corner nook, a huge desk or even a whole room of your own, it could also be a corner of your kitchen, the end of the dining room table, a little desk or chair in your bedroom or living room, or even a drawer or shelf that is all yours. Create the best space you can in your home or office; a space that you love to be in, rest in, dream in, create in and live in.

Make it as decluttered, spacious and beautiful as you can. Only include things that 'bring you joy', as Marie Kondo, author of *Life Changing Magic of Tidying Up*, would say. If an item doesn't bring you joy, discard it, sell it, or give it away, with love and thanks.

Creating a space to create in can support our focus, clarity, energy and productivity on every level: mental, emotional, physical and spiritual. To my mind, the act of creating this space—a sacred sanctuary that is yours—almost feels like a spiritual process, because the world can feel noisy, and having a space to retreat to is nourishing and needed.

How to create your own space
Pick a spot, any spot
Pick a spot in your home or office that is calling out to you. If you need to, make a space. Sell an old piece of furniture and buy something beautiful in its place; move things around until some space appears; clear an edge of the dining room table; tidy up your desk, cupboard, room or wherever your new space will be.

Define its purpose
Is this space to rest, read, write and dream? Is it to write your book? Is it to do the work that calls to you every day? Is it to vision up what's next for you, clear away the old and make space for the new? Be clear on the purpose of your space, so you can enhance it with the appropriate tools and furniture, as well as the right energetic vibration, for what you're calling in.

Fill it with things you love
Get your space ready by filling it with the things you love. For instance, my workspace is filled with my favourite daily planner, plants, essential oils, a diffuser, candles, crystals (amethyst, hematite, citrine and clear quartz are on current rotation), oracle cards, notebooks, pens and Post-its.

Retreat to it, often
This is your space. Use it as and when you need (even if it's just a drawer with all the essentials you love).

Keep it sacred
Try not to use your space to dump the day's stuff or scroll mindlessly through Instagram. Use it with intention and purpose; enjoy being in it. You created it, after all.

Enjoy your space. And as my mum always says when I buy something new, 'I wish you well to use it!'

ALIGNED AND UNSTOPPABLE AFFIRMATION

I joyfully create a beautiful space in which to create, dream and vision, cultivating peace of mind, spaciousness and freedom, so I can do the work I love.

CHAPTER 25

The Resistance

Resistance is directly proportional to love. If you're feeling massive Resistance, the good news is it means there's tremendous love there too. If you didn't love the project that is terrifying you, you wouldn't feel anything.

STEVEN PRESSFIELD, *THE WAR OF ART*

Just before sitting down to write this book, fear nearly got the better of me. This was despite the fact that I knew that this was the next book I'd write—one I had to write, for myself first of all. This fear came up again and again; more fear than I've ever known or felt in relation to any of my work.

It wasn't the fear that said, 'You don't know how to write.' Because I know I do.

It wasn't the fear that said, 'You don't have the time to write.' Because I know I can make the time.

It was the fear that said, 'Who are you to write this book?'

As Marianne Williamson has been quoted and paraphrased so often: *Who are you not to ... ?*

Then I remembered something I read in Steven Pressfield's *The War of Art*, where he said that the more resistance we have towards something, the more fear we have; which means the more we must know that's what we need to do, to evolve and grow on a soul level.

At a soul level, I already knew I had to write this book; but at a mental level, I was resisting. I made up excuses, I bargained with myself, I told myself it didn't matter that much, I told myself not everything I start has to be completed. Nevertheless, the book persisted.

And then I remembered something I teach my students at my writing and creativity workshops:

> *You might not be the only person to write about your topic of choice, but no-one will ever sound like you, when you let yourself use your voice and love what you create.*

I remembered how much I actually thrive when I move through my own resistance. I reconnected with the part of myself that doesn't make excuses about fear, procrastination, resistance, overwhelm or creative insecurities. And so I took my own advice, sat down, and kept writing.

The thing is, I knew this was the next book for me to write. I also knew it didn't matter that I didn't know what the final outcome would look like. How could I? I hadn't even written it yet! So that couldn't be what was stopping me from writing it.

This book pulled at me, tugged at me, and nudged me for months before I wrote it. It would start downloading to me in sentences, just one by one (from the prior experience of having written two books, this is how I know a book is ready to be written).

The more I tried to ignore it or push it aside by saying, 'Maybe I'm not good enough to write this book', the more it tugged at me.

'Who are you kidding?' I heard in reply. 'This is your next book. You can't change that. This book is already within you. This book is already written, somewhere. You're simply making space for it to arrive.'

'Okay, okay. I'll write it!' I said (in defiance and relief). And so, here we are.

It pushes and pulls

What I've found is that there's the resistance that pops up when we're about to sit down and do the work, seemingly pushing us away, and then there's the resistance that pulls us back towards our work when we're trying to walk away from it.

'The work' can be whatever it is you know you're here to do; whatever it is that's calling to you.

The resistance that pushes you away from the work whispers: *You can't.*

The resistance that pulls you towards the work whispers: *Oh, but you must.*

I must. And if you're here, you must too.

It's everywhere

When you're starting something new, when you're building something from the ground up (or even if you're already halfway through), you'll find resistance everywhere, if you look for it:

— If you look for all the ways you can't do something, you'll find them.

— If you look for all the excuses to make, you'll make them.

— If you decide it's too hard (or big, or out of reach), you'll make it too hard (or big, or out of reach).

— If you decide that everyone else has done it before you, you'll keep yourself firmly where you are.
— If you decide there's no space for you, you'll only feel the pinch of 'not enoughness'.

Instead, make space for yourself, rise up, and create it—because you must.

Don't listen to the voice in your head that says you're not good enough to make it, or create it, or be it. Listen to the messages from your heart—the ones that say: *If I don't do this now, when? Why shouldn't it be me? If I can't see I'm ready now, when will I ever be?*

Listen to the messages that say holding yourself back from this will create more tension and turmoil than moving forwards to your light. Listen to the messages that say thinking everyone else has done it before you is simply you keeping yourself small, and undervaluing every single part of yourself.

There is no-one else like you on this planet, so no-one else can create what you will create. No-one else will write like you, or speak like you, or show up like you. No-one.

That was a nudge ... are you listening?

The Universe will guide you, if you're open to it.

I was sitting at my desk, procrastinating. I often joke that I'm not a good procrastinator—it's usually harder to find my 'off' switch than my 'on' switch. However, I had set aside time on this particular day to make progress on this book, and it was now 2.22pm and I'd done everything but write.

Then I got an Instagram message from a woman who'd read one of my books. Her ending remark was: *Can't wait for your next book!*

Now, she couldn't have known that I was writing my 'next book'. At that time, I'd not told anyone except my publisher, my hubby, close family and a handful of girlfriends. (Also, the pinboard above my desk, decorated with Post-its saying, 'I let go of the how' and 'First draft done by X date.')

Reading her words sprung me into action. I closed down my email, jotted down my word count so far (I love keeping track of how many words I write per day), made a huge mug of tea, put on my music, and got to work.

As Elizabeth Gilbert says in *Big Magic*: *The idea will organise coincidences and portents to tumble across your path, to keep your interest keen.*

This happens to me more and more. While writing this book, every time part of my mind and energy was focused on a specific chapter or theme, if I had clients booked in that day, one of them would bring up exactly what I'd been writing about. (That's one reason why there are so many insights and stories from client sessions woven into the fabric of this book.)

I couldn't ignore the ideas coming through to me, and I couldn't ignore this book. You'll find it's the same, for whatever it is you're making. The Universe will support you (if you're open to it). You'll be nudged and prodded. You'll be guided and reminded. You'll realise that you have to sit down and create this, make this, share this. And any feeling of tension, fear, overwhelm, perfectionism or comparison will cease to hold you back, because the idea has more pull. And also because you know that you totally can.

Let's go through some other ideas to help you move through the resistance and into what's next.

Trust it's already within

You can't use up creativity; the more you use, the more you have.
Maya Angelou

Rabbis say we have all our wisdom in the womb; but when we're born the angels ask us to 'shhh' (read that while imagining your pointer finger resting lightly on your lips), which is why we have the indent in our Cupid's bow.

You have all your wisdom within you all the time. You don't need to make it up. You simply need to share what you already know, what you're uncovering, what you're deepening, what you're expanding into. I'm sure the angels won't mind! *wink, wink*

When you trust that it's already within, you get to lean into the resistance, instead of the fear. And when you lean into the resistance, what you're really leaning into is love. All love.

Just let it be good

And now that you don't have to be perfect, you can be good.
John Steinbeck

Resistance will tell you it has to be perfect, or it's not worth it.

But surely, you realise by now that there's no such thing as perfection? Surely you'll let yourself do what you love, and let it be good, and let that be more than enough?

Carve out time to create, and then honour it

The capacity to lock onto a dream and tune out distractions is the difference between an idea and an empire.
Danielle LaPorte

We must call out the resistance, create the time to create, and honour it. If a room (or a space) of our own is important for us to write and create, then so is another kind of space: the mental space that is provided when we carve out time to create—to do the work that lights us up.

One way we can do this is to prepare to create by clearing our mind and creating white space, because making space to create is one of the keys to actually creating.

Sometimes when we want to create something, it can feel so far away. We have this gorgeous, lush, light idea and we want to dive into it, but then life happens. We look ahead to our week and only see snippets of time to create in, but it doesn't feel like it's enough. We feel the resistance that tells us we need more time, and that we'll never have it, so we shouldn't try anyway.

We are the ones who must give ourselves permission to let go of our distractions and commit to our dreams. If you want to make time and space to do something that lights you up, you are the only one in your life who can give you permission for that. So give yourself the permission you're craving and create the space you need, in however many blocks or snippets of time are possible.

What if we flipped our perception of time and creativity on its head? Instead of thinking we are creating our work, what if we understand that it's already created and we are bringing it into form? Let's reverse the creativity process: it's already been created, on some level, in some form, so now you're making space to receive it and bring it to life.

Make time to honour what you need to create and release, and to feel the flow of energy shift mountains in your mind. Make time to do what lights you up from within.

Do the work

When it comes to being aligned and unstoppable, we must call on and ground into our truth and flow, but we must also sit down and do the work. This is when all excuses need to leave the room; any lingering procrastination needs to go; and the things that don't matter need to be put on the backburner.

When I say 'the work', I mean anything that needs your deep focus, your true attention, in order for you to continue mapping out your path.

For me right now, 'the work' is this book. Sometimes it's finishing a new course, writing a talk, brainstorming a new workshop or planning the strategy and launch of a program. Sometimes 'the work' is doing the inner work: clearing blocks and releasing fears; diving deep into what I'm calling in and making space to receive it.

Whatever 'the work' is for you, make it as simple, easy and enjoyable as possible. Let yourself enjoy the sitting down, and you'll let yourself enjoy the work too.

Do it now

Grab your daily planner or calendar, and make the space you're craving for whatever you need most.

If you want to create something new in this world, you need to make space for it to be created. If you know you want to create something new, block your calendar out.

Tell the Universe you're doing this, funnel your energy into it so it happens, and let the resistance transmute into what you need most right now: creative focus, power, purpose and passion.

ALIGNED AND UNSTOPPABLE AFFIRMATION

I lean into the resistance, knowing it's really love guiding me for the evolution and growth of my soul. I easily carve out the time I need, to do the work I love.

CHAPTER 26

It Won't Always Go to Plan

When you're truly aligned to what you're creating, you become unstoppable—even if bumps in the road feel like they're slowing you down. Even if the path becomes twisted, your vision temporarily distorted, your mind temporarily distressed.

You find your flow again because you create it and make it and step into it; because you believe and receive, receive and believe. Because you know you are enough, you trust yourself and your intuition and you know that you've got this (or something even better).

It won't always go to plan; but don't let that stop you.

Keep going when things go pear-shaped

I was once asked by a huge, glossy magazine to do make-up on their editor as a trial. If I got the gig, I'd become one of the magazine's main make-up artists, with consistent, easy work.

I was so nervous—and the editor so chatty—that I became distracted and basically forgot to finish doing her make-up. That sounds ridiculous, because I was experienced and really good at what I did. But when I got home, my stomach sank as I remembered I hadn't put eyeliner on her; and had I even done mascara? Did I add highlighter? What had happened to my brain? I called my agent in a panic. Needless to say, I didn't get the job.

Then there was the time I walked past a retail space for lease and had grand visions of opening my own naturopathic clinic, with Instagram-worthy storefront displays, a healing dispensary and clinic area, and a cool space to host workshops and events. I became obsessed with the idea. I called the real estate agent and set up meetings; I mapped it all out; I started to think through all the details and envision my life with this new space in it. However, the whole thing fell through within weeks. While I was initially very disappointed, I soon realised it would have been the absolutely wrong step for me to take.

A few months later, I moved my entire business to work from home, cutting costs instead of creating new ones. This opened up more availability for online healing and coaching sessions, boosting my flexibility and income. It all worked out in my favour, and for the complete betterment of my business. To this day, when I walk past that retail space I still feel a palpable, physical sense of relief that I didn't sign the contract to take on that lease.

When things don't go to plan, you'll be asked to recommit to your dreams. The view might be a little different to what you hoped for or expected, but when you're truly living in alignment with what you're working towards, and with where you are right now, you'll lean into this new version with even more gusto than before.

JOURNALLING PROMPT

What examples come to mind of things that haven't gone to plan in your life, but have worked out better than you could have anticipated?

ALIGNED AND UNSTOPPABLE AFFIRMATION

*I'm committed to my dreams, and I'm living in alignment
with what I'm working towards, trusting that it'll manifest
in a way that'll serve and support my highest good.*

CHAPTER 27

Create to Heal

*Don't try to figure out what other people want to
hear from you—figure out what you have to say.*

BARBARA KINGSOLVER

When I was in my early twenties, I enrolled in an online creative
writing course. I did this because I loved writing and wanted to
write more, and because I wanted to have a creative outlet for my
writing (apart from my own journal).

It had been several years since I'd left university to pursue my
career as a hair and make-up artist. While I was being creative
through my make-up, I was still craving an extra hit of creativity.
I needed to sit down and write ... I just didn't know what.

But the main reason for enrolling in the writing course was
that I'd just ended a relationship and I felt sad and needed to heal.
I needed to heal through my writing: by using my words to build
me back up; by spending my time in a way that felt nourishing and
built momentum. I needed to feel like I was moving forwards in my
life, not wallowing in the sadness of a relationship that was over.

I enrolled, as nervous and excited as a little schoolgirl on her
way to big school.

I didn't know anyone in the course, but as it was run purely online, I didn't feel the nerves I may have felt if I'd had to walk into a building where I didn't know a soul. The extent of my online interaction was giving weekly feedback on the work of two of my classmates, which was easy enough in my semi-fragile state.

The truth is, while I was joining a group of writers, I didn't really want to make friends. That sounds selfish, I know, but mostly I wanted to write for myself. I wanted to lift myself up through words of fiction; I wanted to create something out of nothing, for no reason at all, except the meaning I placed on my own work.

That was many years ago—over a decade in fact—and so I don't remember what I wrote. But what I do remember is the pure, deep, inner joy I felt at making tea, padding down the carpeted hallway, walking into my bedroom, closing the door softly behind me and sitting down to write, for absolutely no-one but myself.

Do it for yourself

In kinesiology—and energetic, metaphysical medicine—we understand that we hold stored emotions and memories in our bodies. Part of my work as a kinesiologist and healer is to help clients release these to help them move forwards.

Now, if you believe this on any level—that we can hold rage, anger, pain and grief inside our bodies—you'll also believe the flip side: that we can hold love, joy, peace and contentment inside too.

My memory of sitting down to write and create, for the pure joy of it, for myself first, for my own healing, for my own need and desire ... well, that's stored inside me. So when I go to sit down and write, I reactivate that memory deep within. Although I initially booked into that writing course to heal from a break-up, I did it for myself. And I did it with love for myself.

And so that's one of my favourite, most treasured memories of writing—because I wrote for myself, first. Even though I felt sad, I showed up for myself and found I could write with joy. I wrote with no-one else. I wrote for no-one else. And funnily enough, I wrote fiction. (Okay, confession time! I secretly dream of writing a novel one day—perhaps I'll come full circle.)

If you want to sit down and love what you create, you have to make it a habit to actually sit down and write—or create—for yourself, first.

Too many of my clients struggle to sit down and get going, because they're still wondering who they're writing to, or what they're creating.

It's said that you should write what you know, and I agree of course. But I also believe that writing what you know isn't the only way to write. In the same vein, I believe we can create (whatever it is your heart calls for you to make) to heal, for ourselves first.

Don't think about anyone else yet. Create for yourself, first.

You can write to understand what has happened, where you are now, where you're going, and how you'll get there.

You can create what you know, and what you want to believe.

You can paint about what confuses and perplexes you.

You can start something that lights you up.

You can make something in order to heal, or to rise, or to go deeper.

You can compose what you want to understand more.

You can create from your heart, from your soul, from your inner guide and wisdom, from your highest self.

You can produce something about what you've just discovered, and about what you've always known.

You can create what you love, first.

You can create because you need to; you can create because you want to.

You can write because you have to; because if you don't, the words you don't say will burn a mark on your heart and you'll always wonder ... what if?

You can write because you might show it to everyone or to no-one.

You can write because writing about it is how you grow and expand, how you clear and release, how you strategise and plan, how you take action and receive, how you make your mark, how you show up for yourself, and how you serve others.

And also, perhaps most importantly, you can write—and create and make and share—because. Just because.

ALIGNED AND UNSTOPPABLE AFFIRMATION

I create to heal, to discover, to grow and to expand. I let myself create because I love it, and I love what I create because I let myself do so.

CHAPTER 28

Let Your Powers Combine

Nutrition and naturopathy are how my business began; the rest of the story is how it evolved.

To write this book, I had to step up and play bigger and say: *I help women in their lives, but I also deeply help them in their business, creativity, work, path, purpose and passions* (which, in turn, helps them in their lives).

I'd been doing this work for years, but as I've mentioned, it was a pivot from my original work. There were times I still felt like I had to justify this, even though—as you now know too—it's your business, your work, your soul-based path, and your choice.

I had to stop thinking I could split the two: life alignment work and business alignment work.

I had to use all my gifts, blend all my passions, and stop trying to fit myself into a box built by ... who?

Combining your passions and your powers

Did you ever watch Captain Planet when you were little? *By your powers combined, I am Captain Planet!*

For some (perfect) reason, the theme song to this children's TV show popped into my head when I was thinking about this chapter. So my questions to you are:

Are you trying to segregate, split and compartmentalise your passions?

Are you constantly trying to fit into a box made by someone else?

Are you toning down what you do, or watering down the skills you have, because you're worried they don't all 'fit perfectly'?

It's when your passions and powers are combined that you are most powerful.

For so long, I tried to focus on one or the other, extinguishing part of my passions (and myself) in the process. Instead of using fire to heat the flow of my life, I watered it down, and what was left was lukewarm. This became exhausting and confusing, because if the deepest parts of ourselves speak up and we're not listening, then after a while we stop listening to our dreams.

There was a period when I felt overwhelmed and confused, because of my multi-passionate career. I wondered if I was on the right path and if I should radically change my business, work and life path. Should I throw in the towel? Scrap everything I'd worked on? Rebrand? But other avenues felt muddy and confusing, and not in alignment with where I was. After some time, I realised why.

When I'm doing make-up (which I still do, from time to time), the clients who have no idea what they want are often the hardest to work with (I say that in a loving way). If you don't know what you want, nothing makes you happy. They'll say they think they kinda maybe sorta want a smoky eye; so you do a smoky eye and then they ask for a nude shadow. They'll say they think they sorta maybe kinda want a bright lip; so you do a red lip and then they say they prefer a peach gloss. Do this, they want that. They say they'll know what they like when they see it, but I think it's the other way around. You have to know what you like to find it.

How can you radically change what you've already created, if you're not sure what you want to create moving forward?

I decided that making a huge change when I was feeling stressed, ungrounded (and possibly slightly irrational) was not the smartest idea. And so I waited.

And that was when I realised I didn't have to radically change anything on the outside; I had to change from within. I had to declare what I did fearlessly, and to myself first. I had to let myself believe that I was worthy and capable and that this work—the blending of all I do and all I love—was my soul work.

So I decided to let myself combine what I love in a way that works for me, and in a way that supports my passions, powers and purpose, ensuring I'm supporting my clients—and myself—as best I can. I decided to stop worrying about what everyone else was thinking, and claim what worked for me.

Blending your gifts

I started my entrepreneurial career as a hair and make-up artist. I worked my butt off, assisting top make-up artists (usually for free). I'd been told it usually took several years to get an agent, but in just over a year I had signed with an incredible hair and make-up agency. They managed my jobs and bookings, payments and clients. I couldn't have been more excited.

Working as a freelancer meant no two days were ever the same. I didn't have an office to go to, instead many different studios and outdoor locations across Sydney. Almost every day, I was working with new people who often became part of a crew of rotating photographers, hairdressers (if I wasn't also booked to do the hair), stylists, creative directors, clients and models.

Meeting new people most days meant I had to be great at turning strangers into friends quickly, and balancing my intro-verted and extroverted self. This helped me make the 'jump' from make-up artist to nutritionist and naturopath, because I already knew how to find clients, work with new people, make people (and myself) feel comfortable in a new setting, and work in a freelance capacity.

As I've mentioned, I'd also been writing for most of my life. So one way I could combine my skills was by blending my writing, freelance make-up skills and entrepreneurial skills in my business.

All of that experience, all of those skills that I've honed and crafted over the years, continue to help me in my business and life today. If I'd tried to compartmentalise one skill, I'd have made things harder for myself. If I'd ignored one, or hidden one, I wouldn't be here writing this book now.

It's time to take action
Own your gifts
Play with the notion of owning all your gifts and passions throughout life and work; stop compartmentalising, yielding, hiding, staying small or making excuses for what you do, why you do it, why you love it, and how it helps your heart.

Speak up about what you do
Talk about how you can help people, and how you're serving the world by blending all your gifts. Together, your resilience, gifts, strength and passion are greater than the sum of their parts.

Acknowledge how far you've come

You didn't get here by accident or luck. We're so used to looking ahead that we can forget to be grateful for—and proud of—every step that's brought us here. To do that, we have to let ourselves acknowledge the courage that we have already developed to be able to stand here today.

And all the while, keep coming back to what you love the most; keep letting yourself adjust, evolve and course-correct as needed; and keep reminding yourself that you've got what it takes to create what you most desire (or something better).

An essence for alignment

Wild Oat is an ideal Bach flower essence to use here, as it supports you in finding your true path, even if it feels somewhat murky and confusing at first. It'll help you to find the best direction to take, in relation to your ambitions and dreams.

You may also like to take Scleranthus essence to help you work with your intuition, especially if you need to feel clearer in your decision-making process (e.g. if you constantly swing between decision A or B).

ALIGNED AND UNSTOPPABLE AFFIRMATION

I trust it's safe and easy for me to blend all my gifts, skills and talents to step into my most powerful, aligned and grounded self.

CHAPTER 29

The Deepest Connection

You may have heard writers speak about 'the flow'. This refers to the state you enter when you're deep in your writing and creating; when the words flow out of you, through you, as if written elsewhere and simply (beautifully) being downloaded to you.

This flow is accessible to us all, in many different forms. It helps us to conjure and create what we're calling in next, and to feel connected to source, energy, ideas and inspiration.

You can find your flow by deepening your connection to yourself, your body, your energy system, your intuition, the Universe, and your Guides.

To help you tap into a deep connection, imagine sending a mental note or energetic email—asking something, confirming something, perhaps requesting help or support—to your Guides, the Universe, your intuition, or to your own inner wisdom and source of information.

In response, you may feel this information, see it, hear it, sense it or intuit it. You may receive insights and answers through your body; seeing, hearing or feeling the answers you receive. Words or images might drop in, or you might wonder whether you've just made up the answer yourself. Whatever response you receive, tune in. If it feels right—if it feels expansive—trust it and go with it.

For me, the flow feels slightly different to receiving direct insight and answers from my Guides or intuition, but it comes from the same universal source of something deeper and higher than my physical body.

So next time you're sitting down to write or create, if you feel like you have no idea what you're doing, or you wonder if the timing is right, or you don't know if you should go this way or that, then tune in. Close your eyes and take a deep breath, in and out. Let the deepest connection guide you on how to take the next best step.

You don't need to know the 'how'

What if I told you that while working towards your dreams and creating what you feel drawn to create, you don't need to know the 'how'?

What if I told you that when you try to micromanage every single part of your life and work (which we all do, when our perfectionist self comes to the party too early and you have to entertain her without any other guests around to keep her busy) you actually hold yourself back?

Instead, what if you allowed yourself to trust (and enjoy) the process; to know that, while you can figure out the tough stuff, you can't always know the 'how' of the awe-inspiring synchronicities, the magic, the miracles that come your way?

I sometimes look back on situations that have transpired in an incredible way I couldn't have foreseen, and thank the heavens that I hadn't been in charge of writing that ending, that outcome. Because if I had been, it wouldn't have been nearly as wonderful.

And yes, this works at the opposite end of the spectrum too. Sometimes things just go completely off kilter, so far away from your plan that you feel like you've lost a sense of yourself.

The beauty in letting go of the 'how' is that you allow yourself to be supported by the magic of creativity and the source of universal energy and flow; by something bigger than yourself; by the energy that holds your dreams in place while you work towards them, day by day.

There've been times when I've set a goal, done my best to figure it out, done the work, showed up, but still not known the outcome, or exactly how it would all play out. But I've let myself release my expectations, and those are the times I've felt the most joy.

I let myself do this consistently. When I sit down to write my books, I don't know how they'll turn out. When I create something new, I don't know how it'll turn out. When I set a goal in my business or life, I have no idea how it'll turn out.

When I make big, bold, beautiful plans, I have no idea how things will fall into place. But I show up anyway.

You might not get what you want. It might all go in a completely different direction. It might not turn out how you expected … and that might be the best thing that could happen.

The deepest connection

Cultivating the deepest connection requires a combination of:

Trust

Trust it's all within your reach and capabilities. You don't need to do anything extra in order to tune into the guidance and flow that's always available from within, above and below.

Devotion

Take care with your dreams and your drive. Stay devoted to what's important to you, and self-doubts will soften.

Commitment

Commit to this connection; to receiving it, to asking for it, and to using it for the greater good.

Patience

Don't rush it. You can't anyway (ha!), so funnel that energy into something more important: showing up for yourself and trusting the energy of what you're creating.

Meditation

Meditate on it, focus on it, draw it in. Clear your mind of the clutter, then when guidance and flow drop in, you can recognise and receive this.

Intention

Let your intention be pure and strong. Ask for what you want. You're allowed to. Sit in the embodiment of what you're calling in. You know how.

Gratitude

Be grateful for each moment of flow you cultivate, receive and hold. Thank it, and let yourself ask for more.

Space

Create space to do your best work, to ask for support from something higher, deeper, greater. Then allow yourself to receive it.

When you let go of the 'how', you get to invest your energy where it matters most. Don't focus on events you can't control; focus instead on the events, actions, mindset and energy that keep you in your power, that keep you on your path, that keep you focused.

When you show up with an open heart and mind, when you align your thoughts and energy to where they matter most, then you can stay in your flow, drawing what you desire (or something better) towards you, and letting the 'how' work itself out. You have way more important things to do anyway.

Crystals for alignment

— Amethyst helps you stay connected to your intuition and bigger vision.
— Clear quartz supports you in receiving divine guidance, clarity, inspiration, focus and flow.
— Fluorite supports mental mastery, clarity and focus (I often keep this beautiful crystal close by while writing).

ALIGNED AND UNSTOPPABLE AFFIRMATION

I know I am always able to cultivate the deepest connection, to support me as I step into flow and alignment with my work, path and life.

Part 4

THE QUIET WORK
Self-Care and Self-Belief

CHAPTER 30

Honour Your Own Rhythm

Ah, you're here ... where you've done the inner work, the deeper work and the creative work. And now? Now you must create a beautiful foundation to sustain this work, by honouring your body to fuel your creativity, energy and mindset.

Think of these next few chapters as a toolkit for supporting your focus, activating and restoring your energy, uplifting your mindset, and cultivating deeper habits for self-nourishment and sustainable creativity.

When it comes to being aligned and unstoppable, we have to look at—and look after—all parts of our being. When we focus on our physical, mental, emotional and spiritual wellness, we focus on what energises us so we can do our best work, in all areas of our lives.

When you're putting yourself into your work, and when you're putting your work out there, you have to be clear in mind, body, spirit and soul, and this means looking after yourself on every level.

You will become a better channel and vessel for your work when you're energetically clear, when you slow down and look after yourself, and when you trust that—no matter how much 'work' you've gotten done—you're still enough, and are always allowed to rest when you need it. (And even before you need it.)

There's a rhythm to how you create. Some days the rhythm shows up in full force, in flow, and sometimes it shows up by asking you to slow down and work less. If you try to push through and ignore the rhythm, you can burn out, you can fall out of love with your work, and you can think you're never doing enough.

When I was studying make-up, my teacher once scolded me for finishing a make-up look too quickly. 'Did I do it incorrectly? Does it not look good? Am I on the wrong track with it?' I asked. My teacher shook her head. While it looked great, by her standards I'd gone too quickly.

I couldn't understand this logic. If I'd done a crappy job, if the foundation had been the wrong shade, the eyeliner wobbly, the eye shadow not blended well, the lashes clumpy and the eyebrows wonky, sure, scold me for rushing. But the truth is, the make-up was great and I hadn't rushed. I just work quickly.

That pace only ever served to help me during my make-up career in fashion and beauty, and when doing make-up for private clients. No-one wants a slow make-up artist behind the scenes of a fashion show; or doing make-up for eight people before a wedding; or at a shoot when there are several hair and make-up looks to create and shoot in just a few hours.

Years after that make-up class, I still remembered my teacher's words and obvious annoyance. But I didn't listen to her, because I was simply honouring my own rhythm.

Likewise, when at school I used to be one of the first in my year to finish writing exams. I'd finish the paper, go back from the beginning to check my answers, then put my head down on my desk and rest—sometimes for 45 minutes before the exam ended. I wasn't rushing. I hadn't left out any questions. I hadn't skimped on my essay, or written short answers for long questions.

I was simply honouring my own rhythm.

When I go to art classes, I often finish my paintings before others in my class. The last time I attended art class, I painted five canvases (some oil, some acrylic) in one term of art, when most of my art friends painted one canvas. I wasn't doing a bad job or not finishing my art. I wasn't getting bored before I'd finished. I was simply honouring my own rhythm.

Of course there have been times when I've rushed my work, but I've discovered that the more you honour your own rhythm—while trusting in divine timing, in the bigger picture, and in your greater vision—the less you rush your art, and the less you burn out on your way to creating. This allows you to create and release with pace, without feeling a need to rush.

Honour the way you work best

Let's start honouring our natural rhythms and cycles. You might go slowly, and need time. You might go faster, sprinting to the finish line. You might do both, depending on what you're working on, or yo-yo between the two. Don't judge how you create; celebrate that you do create.

Soon we'll talk about honouring your rhythm on a different level to avoid burnout, but what I'm talking about here is following and honouring the rhythm of your creativity.

I find that each project I work on has an energy, a rhythm, a cycle to follow. Each book I've written has had its own timeline that it whispers to me between the pages I write; each online course I've created has its own rhythm that it communicates to me through scribbled brainstorming sessions in my notebook; each workshop I've held has its own cycle, from conceiving it, to planning it, to creating it, to practising it, to teaching it.

Each piece of work you create, everything you make, will have its own energy, cycle, rhythm, timing and feel. You need to honour this, so that you're creating in—and with—alignment.

To do this, you simply need to listen. Listen to your body, to your guidance, and to the work you're creating. If you listen, it'll tell you when it's ready to be made and when it needs a break (or when it needs you to have a break). It'll tell you when you need a day off, when you need to put it to the side, and when you need to sit down, tune in, turn your phone off and do the work.

It'll tell you its timeline too. As I've mentioned, my books start coming to me in drips, sentences here and there, that I hurriedly type into an Evernote folder (each book has its own 'Notebook' in Evernote) before I forget, before it leaves me. I do this for a while—for as long as the book wants me to—until I know it's time to start writing it. I know when it's time to start writing, because all of sudden, I can't not write it. It's an urge that comes through asking me to do the work, because I need to.

Avoiding burnout

We can do the work when we need and want to, but we also have to allow ourselves to truly rest and restore in between.

In the early years of my business, I'd rest and restore in short, sharp breaks with the focused intention of restoring my energy, so that I could work again (and often, harder). I remember having a mentoring session with an energy healer and coach who suggested I rest and restore for my energy's sake, and not with the intention of restoring it just to create more. I could restore my energy, to restore my energy.

This simple mindset shift changed the way I work. I stopped thinking I had to refuel, simply to go faster and harder. I started to refuel for myself, honouring my own rhythm in a more aligned and more purposeful way. This was one of the first steps I took to heal from the burnout I was creating within myself and my life.

To honour your own rhythm:

— Don't rush for the sake of rushing. Listen to your work and don't let comparison, a sense of lack, or a fear of not being enough stress you into thinking you need to be on a different timeline.

— Don't pause or procrastinate for no good reason. Tune into the timing of what you're working towards and honour it.

— Support yourself along the way, resting and restoring your energy for your energy's sake—not necessarily to energise you to create more. Let this be a cycle that supports you, no matter what's going on elsewhere.

JOURNALLING PROMPTS

— Where or how are you not honouring your own rhythm?
— What shifts and changes can you implement, so that you can honour your own rhythm?
— What would this look like for you (e.g. your ideal morning/day/week of working in this way)?
— How would working like this feel different to the way you currently work?

ALIGNED AND UNSTOPPABLE AFFIRMATION

I honour the rhythm of what and how I create, letting myself stop and refuel, to fully support myself and my dreams.

CHAPTER 31

Honour Your Body

Another way we support our own rhythm in becoming aligned and unstoppable is by honouring our bodies.

One of my lovely clients, Stella—a healer and coach—was trying to navigate the waters of building her business and managing her energy levels, having experienced fatigue during the past few years. For her to do this, she had to become aware of when she was feeling the regular old resistance that we all feel at times, and when she was feeling fatigue—because they are not the same thing.

Fatigue isn't the same as laziness or resistance. Fatigue is a call to activate your self-care. Not just by having a bath or a pedicure, but by letting yourself really slow down, tune in, rest, sleep and nourish to restore your energy.

For you to become aligned and unstoppable, you need to be able to check in with yourself and your energy levels regularly. You need to trust that by slowing down, you're not falling off the wagon—you're feeding the horse that pulls it.

Maintain your flow by letting yourself slow.

The world doesn't need the burnt out, exhausted, stressed version of you. The world needs the version of you who can sit down and do the work, and also step back and rest up. This is the version of you who can do your best work, in a consistent way.

We created goals to align Stella to the way she wanted to work (by honouring her own energy and cycles): letting her do what works for her; pushing through resistance but moving through fatigue; allowing her to take the pressure off herself and see everything she was doing as a fun experiment; and knowing that 'done' is better than 'perfect' (especially when 'perfect' means nothing gets done).

We also aligned her to these specific goals:
— Letting go of perfectionism allows me to flow and be creative.
— Being creative restores and ignites my energy source.
— I believe in myself and my work.
— I embody freedom, ease and flow in my work.
— I allow things to be easy.

After creating these goals together, what came up was a block at her Solar Plexus chakra. This chakra relates to our energy centre, sense of identity, and the centre of our personal power, self-confidence and self-worth.

'Do you trust that you're still worthy of receiving, even if you've slowed down and given yourself time off?' I asked Stella.

'Hmmm,' was her response, with a half-smile and a twinkle in her eyes.

This was at the crux of the session. If we feel that we're not worthy, willing or able to receive unless we're working ourselves to the bone, we're not creating a sustainable way of working or living.

When you look after yourself well, you live in a way that allows you to do your best work and to share your gifts, without burning yourself out or giving too much to others.

Don't be the cliché

We all know the 'artist' cliché: someone who forgets to eat when in their 'creative cave'; who never leaves the house, never eats fresh food, and who forgets to shower, brush their teeth or wash their hair for days on end, all in the name of getting the job done.

I'll be really honest ... ugh! I couldn't think of anything worse for my creativity, energy and mindset than doing (or rather forgetting to do) any of that.

For me, honouring my body is just one way I honour and fuel my creativity. My 'creative cave' is full of fresh air, light, mugs of tea, moving my body, eating well, supporting my body with herbal medicine, taking breaks, having naps, listening to my intuition, going into deep, full flow and also resting and restoring my energy.

I know I do my best work when I care for myself in this way: when I move my body, eat well, breathe fresh air and enjoy breaks. While there are days when, sure, I need to use dry shampoo, I don't forget to look after myself, in the name of looking after my muse.

If you move your body, you'll be more focused, feel calmer, concentrate better (and for longer periods) and undo some of the effects of sitting all day. If you eat well, you'll be fuelling your mind with the nutrients it needs to help you focus, think clearly, and stay alert. If you feel good within yourself, you'll extend that into your work.

Supporting your mood, mindset, creativity and energy is so much easier when your body is nourished and supported. I also believe that when we eat better, healthier foods, we feel more in tune with our bodies, which in turn fuels our creativity, and supports us in listening to our natural rhythms and cycles.

It's not a badge of honour to dive into a cave where you don't support yourself. Instead, create a retreat for yourself, where doing your best work is easier, because you're doing your best for your body, mind, spirit and soul.

Eating to support creativity

Let's talk about which herbs, nutrients and foods will support your mood, creativity and energy. I'm not going to give you a specific meal plan, or tell you what you need to eat and when. I simply want you to listen to your body, and eat healthy, nourishing foods that you know—deep down—are really supporting you.

I'm not saying I've never sat at my desk, deep in my work, and pushed back eating breakfast by hours. I'm not saying I've never eaten lunch close to 4pm, because I've been in flow and haven't noticed the time. I absolutely have. But I always make sure that whether I've carved out time to do deep work, or I'm just going about my daily life and work, I make time to eat good food.

If it means you have to set a timer, to remind you to drink more water and eat something healthy, do that. If it means you have to batch cook some food on the weekend so the fridge is full, do that.

If it means you eat the same breakfast every day for a week, because it's easy and fills you up and lets you focus well, do that. If it means you have to go out for lunch because the fridge is empty, do that.

Just ensure you're looking after yourself and supporting your energy and mood, because it's one simple way to ensure you can continue to show up for yourself and your work.

My favourite herbs to boost mood, energy, focus and creativity

When I think about herbs to support creativity, what I'm really thinking about are herbs to support energy, mood and focus. The rest—calling in your muse, sitting down to do the work whether she shows up or not, showing up and speaking up—will come from the support you provide for yourself, the permission you give yourself, and the actions you take.

When you think of taking herbs in that way, one of the aims is to nourish your adrenals glands and nervous system, build up your vitality and resilience, and support your mood and sleep.

A lot of the following herbs are adaptogenic: they help to support the body's ability to manage stresses and stressors of all kinds. There are also nervine herbs to support and calm the nervous system, and herbs that will help reduce inflammation, manage cortisol levels and generally heal and support the adrenal glands to support energy, general wellbeing and hormonal health.

You can drink some of them as teas (e.g. chamomile, passionflower, licorice) and/or you can find them in liquid and tablet forms in all good health food stores. Instead of self-prescribing, please make sure you pop into a health food store and ask a qualified naturopath or herbalist (not a nutritionist—they're not trained in herbal medicine) if they believe these herbs will suit you. (Please also tell them if you're pregnant, breastfeeding or trying to conceive, are on any medication/s or have any allergies.)

Rhodiola is one of my favourite herbs (you may already know that, if you've read my previous books). It'll support your energy, mood, focus, immune system and hormones. It'll increase your physical and mental endurance and stamina, as well as support a healthy mood. No kidding, it is my go-to herb for life!

Bacopa and **Ginkgo** are two great herbs for focus and mood. Bacopa calms anxiety while improving cognition, helping you to feel calm and in the zone. Ginkgo promotes antioxidant and anti-inflammatory activity, and can reduce stress, increase your mood and support your immune system.

Licorice and **Rehmannia** are two beautiful herbs, traditionally used in combination, which heal and nourish the adrenal glands. Licorice is an amazing herb to support your adrenal health; it helps to modulate stress, increase energy and endurance, and acts as a tonic for the whole body. It can also help balance blood sugar levels and reduce sugar cravings. Rehmannia helps to nourish the adrenals, and acts as a tonic for the adrenals too; it increases energy, reduces inflammation, and cools down the body. It's also great for sugar cravings, dizziness and weakness. You can take these two herbs separately or in combination.

Withania (also called Ashwaganda or Indian ginseng) is a beautiful Ayurdevic adaptogenic herb that helps to heal the adrenals and tonify the body. As an adaptogen, it helps the body adapt. For example, if cortisol is too high, Withania will help to lower it; if cortisol is too low, Withania will help bring it up. It also strengthens all kinds of weaknesses and is wonderful if you've come out of a long period of stress or illness. It will help to reduce inflammation, anxiety, and aches and pains, all while supporting immunity, mood and cognition, as well as strengthening the entire energy system. A winner!

St John's Wort is another go-to if you need mood and nervous system support. It'll support depression, anxiety, stress, irritability and insomnia. (Definitely one to check out with a naturopath/ herbalist before taking, as it can interact with certain medications, including anti-depressants and the contraceptive pill.)

Siberian ginseng is another beautiful adaptogen, that helps to support and rejuvenate the adrenals and the body's energy system. It can increase immunity, support your stress response, normalise metabolism and regulate neurotransmitters (supporting your mood and nervous system). It's great for anyone healing from burnout and fatigue.

Panax ginseng (also known as Korean ginseng) and **American ginseng** are also very healing and supportive herbs. Panax is energising, and supports your cognition, focus and immune system. American ginseng is more calming rather than stimulating, so is another great herb to take to improve your mood, focus and calm the nervous system.

Calming and nervine herbs such as **Chamomile, Passionflower, Lavender, Vervain, Valerian, Skullcap and Lemon Balm** are great if you're feeling stressed, anxious, irritable or finding it hard to sleep.

This is just a snapshot of some of the beautiful herbs that will support your mood, focus and energy. As I've said, please chat to a naturopath or herbalist for more information on a personalised herbal medicine formula for you.

Your wellness is key

You have free will—the choice to decide how you'll look after yourself, and what you'll tell yourself when you do.

So, will you guilt yourself into it? Or will you allow yourself to call your energy back through rest, honouring your own energy, your natural cycles, and through creating a new—and deeply supportive—way of working and being?

ALIGNED AND UNSTOPPABLE AFFIRMATION

*I look after myself in the best way possible, supporting
my energy, flow, creativity and focus. It is safe and
easy for me to nurture, nourish and honour my
body, and I do so with joy, love and gratitude.*

CHAPTER 32

Boundaries, Brain Holidays and Burnout

Don't just do something, sit there.

THICH NHAT HANH, *HOW TO SIT*

We've talked about honouring our creative rhythm and our bodies. Now we must deepen this further by honouring our boundaries and creating brain holidays, so that we don't burn out.

Brain holidays can be as long as weeks off, or as short as a walk around the block in between doing your work. They are really important, if you want to love what you create in a sustainable way. It's in those spaces in between when we relax our minds, that we make space for the answers to flow to us, without pushing, without grinding our teeth, and without stressing ourselves out.

Next time you feel tired, drained or as if your creative mojo has left for a holiday in Mexico (without you, whyyy?), remember that your best ideas will often come when you least expect it; when you're rested, calm and connected; when you're giving yourself time to invest in self-care (which doesn't have to be indulgent at all); and when you're slowing down, tuning out or turning inwards.

You're allowed to not work every day. You're allowed to say 'no thanks'. You're allowed to slow down.

You're allowed to ... but you have to let yourself first.

You're doing enough

By now, we all know that filling our days with too much is a trap; it keeps us stuck. It's the opposite of becoming aligned and unstoppable.

Being busy can be seen as a badge of honour; a sign we wear to show the world we're on the right track. We think that the only way to make stuff happen in our life is to hustle to the point of fatigue, to say 'yes' to every and any opportunity that comes our way, and to put everyone else's needs above our own.

And when we do let ourselves slow down, all too often this can bring up feelings of guilt, fear, betrayal and low self-worth. We worry that we're not good enough, if we're not doing all the things, all the time.

We worry that we'll miss out on opportunities if we're not constantly reaching out and grabbing them, instead of trusting that things will still flow to us in the spaces in between; that we can attract opportunities to us without having to burn out.

We worry about what will happen if we aren't seen to be overly busy, stressing, rushing and frantic. *Maybe people will think I'm not actually working*, you erroneously tell yourself. *Maybe people won't think I'm good enough. Maybe I won't think I'm good enough. Maybe everything I've worked so hard for will come crashing down around me.*

But the first truth is that being busy all the time, every week, every day, every moment, is exhausting. And the second truth is that pushing yourself to exhaustion is often a conscious choice, driven by subconscious fears.

What's another (better) conscious choice? Creating a new, deeply aligned rhythm that supports your mood, energy, creativity and dreams; a rhythm that adapts in a way that continually serves and supports you.

Busyness can hold you back

Pushing yourself to exhaustion keeps you feeling stuck and trapped, always feeling rushed and pressed for time, and as if you're never doing enough.

Excessive and all-consuming busyness holds you back from enjoying all areas of your life, from being the best version of yourself, and from seeing the bigger picture. It will make you feel rushed, as if you're not on the right path. It can exacerbate feelings of failure and disconnect you from your core, your guidance and your path.

I'm not asking you to find the all-elusive 'balance'—some days and weeks, indeed some seasons of your life, are definitely going to be busier and fuller than others. I'm simply asking you to ensure you're looking after yourself in the best way you can, in a way that serves and supports you as you work towards what's next.

A part of me used to think that if I wasn't constantly working on something or moving forwards towards a goal, I was stuck and stagnant. What was I even doing with my life?

That way of thinking is pressurising and draining. And if I'm honest, it came from a place of insecurity. I was worried that if I wasn't always moving ahead and doing more, then I wouldn't become successful, or hit my goals, or feel a sense of achievement.

That kind of thinking is way off the mark. It leads to guilt, fatigue, burnout and ... chocolate. Not my kind of wants (except maybe some chocolate). I'd go for respect over guilt, vitality over fatigue, and ability over burnout, any day (in fact, every day).

It's time to stop filling your days with busyness, and to create and honour your new rhythm instead.

Self-care is not a buzzword

At the peak of my busyness, I didn't even allow one afternoon of doing nothing, let alone a day. I thought that if I had a lot of work to do, that's all I was allowed to do until I had finished it. I wouldn't let myself relax, or go to a midmorning yoga class, or make lunch plans with a friend.

It was exhausting, all that planning and doing, stressing and gripping, with not nearly enough resting, flowing, and trusting.

The key to making self-care feel like a pleasure—without the guilt—is to not see it as something you do randomly, but as a way of living, where you care for yourself daily. Don't see 'self-care' as a buzzword, see it as a way of life.

One way to start is by doing something to bring you joy every day. Write a list of things you love to do, from reading a novel or newspaper, to going to yoga, to cooking dinner with the music pumping, to going to sleep earlier, eating better food, doing a short meditation, eating lunch outside in the sunshine, exercising more consistently, or anything and everything in between. There are no rules here, just whatever brings you joy and makes you feel nourished, connected and calm.

Now, aim to do one thing from your list every day. It might be just half an hour of chill time, but if you block out the time and fill it with what you need most, you'll let yourself fill your cup in the way that'll best support your soul goals and your energy.

You'll also see that you don't need to be constantly working and hustling to draw your dreams closer towards you.

Identify your time and energy leaks

Release what's draining you, by uncovering where you're leaking time and energy.

— Do you find yourself leaking energy when you're around certain people?

— Are you checking social media a million times a day?

— Are you watching boring TV shows, when you could be reading a great novel?

— Do you waste time sitting at your desk being unproductive, when you'd be better off taking a break, going for a walk around the block, then coming back to your tasks with renewed focus and energy?

— Do you go into your inbox every hour and write long replies, when you could be checking your inbox less, and writing your replies in just a few short sentences?

Where are you leaking time? And what could you be doing with your time and energy instead?

Give yourself permission to slow down

If you have a busy job and a full life (which most of us do), you are the only person who can give yourself permission to slow down. This has to be a conscious choice—and it's your conscious choice—so carve out the time you need and honour it.

The only person who can permit you to slow down is you. If you give yourself permission to do so, and you start to see how it positively impacts on your energy and on those around you, you'll be motivated and inspired to carry on looking after yourself in the way that supports you most.

Back yourself

If you make a plan to do some work in the morning, or go to a yoga class, or spend a few hours chilling on your own, or even just have a hot cup of tea at the end of the day after the kids are asleep, you have to back yourself.

Think of it like this: if you made an arrangement with a girl-friend, would you cancel on her ten minutes before? Probably not.

So think of your own self-care plans in the same way. If you've made a date with yourself to have a nap, or read a book, or go for a walk, or even just to do some work before taking the rest of the weekend off, then back yourself and follow through with your plans.

Don't flake out on yourself. You're the one who'll feel it the most.

Become the boss of yourself

My mum tells a story of when I was little, and playing with one of my friends. My friend's mum approached us while we were playing, and asked me if I wanted to sleep over that night.

I said I didn't, and when she asked why and told me my little friend would love to have me sleep over and play, I confidently told her, 'I'm the boss of me.' I had decided not to sleep over; and I was only three!

When you decide to invest in your own self-care in order to support your energy, you become the boss of yourself again, instead of being bossed around by deadlines, schedules, to-do lists, mental clutter and that constant, cyclic, running list of things you think you should be doing.

Listen to your body more

Instead of just using your head to make decisions, feel into your body.

When thinking about making new plans or jumping into a new project, ask your body for the answer:

— Take a deep, cleansing, calming breath in.
— Ask your body a question.
— Feel into your body: does it feel expansive, open and light? Expansive equals a 'yes'.
— Or does it feel contracted, restricted and heavy? Contracted means 'no'.

Listen to your body, then take action with that wisdom in mind (and heart).

Be honest

When I was healing from burnout years ago, I knew I had to rein in my energy. If I was tired, if I couldn't meet a deadline, if I had to reschedule, or if I needed time alone, I would be honest with myself, and with my family, friends or work contacts.

I didn't want to be a flake, but I knew that looking after my energy and my boundaries was my main priority. I found that being honest with people was much nicer than flaking out.

Sometimes it was as simple as shooting off an email like one of the following:

> Thank you so much, I would love to say 'yes', but I have a lot on my plate right now. Can we get in touch in another couple of weeks?

> Thank you so much. This sounds amazing, but I don't think I'm the right gal for you right now. Instead, I'd love to refer my friend, B, to write a quote for your article.

I would love to be involved, but I'll only be able to get that piece back to you in five days, not two. Let me know if this is okay, otherwise I can refer you to a friend.

By being clear about what you can take on, and when you need to say 'no', you get to manage expectations while you manage your own energy. It's a win-win.

Strengthen your boundaries

Boundaries define your territory. They define what you say 'yes' to and what you say 'no' to. They also teach other people how they should treat you and communicate with you.

Without energetic boundaries, you may say 'yes' when you really want to say 'no'; take on the energy and 'stuff' of others; burn yourself out by giving too much of yourself to others; never allow yourself to put yourself first and do what you need to do. And on and on it goes.

You can't work every moment of every day and still show up in the world as the best version of yourself. You need to set boundaries. You need to take breaks. You need to give yourself time out, and time off. You need to let yourself see that you don't always have to be working, to get to where you want to be.

Harnessing the power to protect your own energy is potent and powerful. Setting clear boundaries that raise your vibration and protect your energy is as simple as setting the intention to do so, then following through with your actions.

To strengthen your boundaries, give yourself permission to:
— Realise it's okay to say 'no'.
— Be okay with looking after your own best interests.

— Allow yourself to release any guilt you feel around saying 'no' and looking after yourself.
— Give yourself hours, days and weekends off.
— Feel into what feels out of alignment in your life, decide how you'd rather feel about it, then make a clear choice about how to move forward in alignment.
— Recognise your limits (time, energy, resources) and if needed, either say, 'Thanks, but no thanks' or 'Sure, but can we do it this way?', asking for help along the way if needed.
— Be clear about when you work, and let yourself really enjoy your time off (without feeling guilty).
— See self-care as a way of living and being, not something you do once in a while.
— Trust in the spaces in between. Things won't fall apart if you slow down and rest.

Creating firm but loving boundaries sets you up for success, and prevents you from feeling burnt out and resentful. The truth is, burning out doesn't make you more successful. It doesn't give you clarity, make you more money, or make you more productive or smarter. Burning out doesn't give you a sense of accomplishment, ease or freedom. In fact, it does the opposite; it prevents you from showing up in the world in the way you're needed most.

When you set boundaries, you are aligning to a new way of working and being that suits you. And your new boundaries will soon feel like a second skin.

Doing less is a conscious choice
You might have to consistently remind yourself that it's okay to do less, to become less busy, and that's okay. It'll get easier and

easier to rest, relax and restore your energy, so you have energy for yourself, those around you, and your dreams.

There'll always be 'stuff' to do: to-do lists to tick off, groceries to be shopped for, laundry to be washed, beds to be made, emails to be replied to, and dogs to be walked. But you have the option of creating less busy time in your life by just declaring it, then making space for it and implementing it with love.

Initially, this might feel strange to you. You might feel guilty, scared, nervous, or like you're just not doing enough. But remember, the world doesn't need the burnt-out, exhausted version of you.

The world needs the strongest, most vibrant version of you—you at your best. And the best version of you is hiding behind that 'being busy' stuff. The stuff that keeps you tied down, distracted and empty. The stuff that keeps you aimlessly busy. The stuff that keeps you running away from relaxing, because you think you need to earn the right to rest.

You don't need to earn the right to rest. You're worthy of it right now.

JOURNALLING PROMPTS

— When do you feel most energised and focused?
— How can you invite more of this into your life and work?
— Where are your boundaries feeling out of whack?
— What do you need to do to create new boundaries, or how can you strengthen/tidy them up?
— When can you schedule some time off?
— What will you do to ensure you honour this time?
— What will you remind yourself, if you start to feel anxious, stressed or worried when you slow down and rest?

— What will you remind yourself, if you start to feel burnt out, exhausted or drained in the future?

ALIGNED AND UNSTOPPABLE AFFIRMATIONS

- *I know I am worthy of slowing down and relaxing.*
- *I let myself enjoy self-care, knowing it's supporting me in every aspect of my life and work.*
- *I give myself permission to let my body, mind and spirit rest, restore and heal.*
- *I know it's safe and easy for me to slow down.*
- *I am ready to allow myself to rest and relax.*
- *I give myself permission to enjoy my time off.*
- *I easily create healthy, firm boundaries that I honour with love.*

Part 5

THE REST OF THE WORK

It's Your Turn Now

CHAPTER 33

You're Always Growing

I've been thinking about growth lately. Specifically, how we can be so hard on ourselves if (or when) we feel like we aren't growing 'enough', or when we feel like we 'should' be further ahead than we are.

There are so many ways we can measure our growth; I've found that to do so by first looking within—so we don't compare, constrict or criticise—can be the most powerful.

Let yourself look at the bigger picture and be proud of what you've accomplished (even when the timeline doesn't quite match up with your 'ideal' timeline). Then you can let yourself enjoy the flow of inner freedom and joy you put in motion when you set a goal/dream/intention, and work towards it as slowly and purposefully as you need to, trusting the outcome without forcing or controlling it.

You can let yourself balance growth with gratitude.

As we create, and look ahead to the horizon of what we wish to move towards in life and work, things will continuously grow, shift and change. Our actions and reactions, our input and output, our internal uplevellings and our external engagements, will continuously reflect where we are in our lives, and what we're needing to deepen, work on, heal, release and let go of.

Sometimes you'll go through a period where your inward shifts will outweigh the outward goals, and you'll have to surrender to these changes. Other times, your energy and focus will be singularly and beautifully directed at one goal, one project, one mission, and you may find yourself surrendering to that deep flow.

I've had to do it myself this year. In real time as I write this, I'm nearly 28 weeks pregnant. From healing from a blighted ovum (a type of miscarriage) at the start of the year, to now entering the third trimester of pregnancy, I can point to where the majority of this year's growth has gone. (Baby girl!) I've surrendered to creating in a new way this year, and although I've tried to push back against this at times, in hindsight I can see it has been perfect.

I became witness to a new way of working, one that allowed me to deepen my flow, honour my own rhythm and respect my body and energy levels more deeply and greatly than ever before.

And so, as I near the end of this book (this book that called on me to deepen, within myself, absolutely everything I've written about in these pages), I've been reflecting on growth. Can we still have it when it looks very different to what we anticipated? I'm loving the answers and insights that are coming through in the process.

Here are some tips to support you, if you're going through a period of growth that might feel sticky, or wanting to reconnect to the part of you who is truly always evolving:

— **Growth is always, always, always available to you**
It's always available to you, even if it looks different to how you imagined. You are never static. And while you can always lean into

your growth and into what's next, raising your energy, vibration and frequency, and growing into who you are, you're also allowed to trust that you're in the right place for yourself, right now.

— **You don't have to control your growth**
In fact, if you try to, you may find yourself feeling further away from it. Rather, allow yourself to align to it in your own time and in your own way, always trusting in the 'or something better'.

— **You can always grow and evolve at your own pace**
Racing and rushing doesn't get you to the finish line faster (because there is no finish line).

— **You can feel expansion and fear at the same time**
The fear will be in your head (hoping you'll grip onto it), the expansion will sit in your body (hoping you'll let go of the fear, waiting for you to lean into what's next). Listen to your body first. And then? Trust, and stay open—knowing you're supported and protected throughout this process of growth. (This time, and the next. And the next. And the next ...)

Lean into the turning point

The more you trust in your growth and evolution, the more you can trust that there'll be a turning point in your journey of activating your creativity and soul gifts.

I don't mean you'll feel the enigma of 'one day', or of being 'there yet', because you'll always be growing and creating, and one day is today. But there'll be a point where something clicks into place for you; it'll feel like a question being answered; black and white turning to colour; the volume turning up.

It'll be a point where self-criticism is more easily transmuted into self-confidence; where you feel like you've unlocked something which was always deeply embedded within.

You'll know you're on the right path, and you'll allow yourself to stop comparing yourself to others, to stop wondering if you're doing enough, to stop thinking you must be missing a memo that everyone else has been alerted to. You'll let yourself claim where you are, and more importantly, who you are.

You'll know how to activate, deepen and call on the creative, magnetic, radiant power that is always—and already—within you.

And it'll happen again and again, as you continue to uplevel, upgrade, do the work, show up, and love what you create.

You'll continue to deepen your work, and honour your gifts. You'll continue to deepen the purpose that fuels your passion, and the passion that fuels the light that you are, the light you spread out into the world.

And as you now know, that light has to come from within first, and be honoured within first.

ALIGNED AND UNSTOPPABLE AFFIRMATION

*I trust in my ability to grow and evolve at my own
pace, knowing I am always supported, and able
to lean into my expansion, evolution and flow.
I activate, deepen and call on the power that is
always and already within me, knowing this supports
me to fuel my passion, purpose and light.*

CHAPTER 34

There's Always Room at the Top

While I was studying make-up, I went to live in Toronto for seven months to attend an international make-up college. I'll never forget what our instructor said to our class of about 25 students (and very new friends) on our first day: 'There might be a lot of you sitting in this room now, and when you graduate, you'll likely all be working in similar circles. But don't let that hold you back; there's always room at the top.'

I'll never forget that phrase: *There's always room at the top.* It means there's always room for good work. There's always room for your work.

Sure, there'll always be someone who does what you do, who's done it for longer, who you think does it better, in some way. But they'll never do it like you, and there is always space for you—if you make it.

To believe there's space for us too, we have to call our energy—and our power—back to ourselves.

We have to have to be grateful for those who've gone before us and shown us the way. We have to have faith and trust in our own life path. We have to have the courage to be happy for those who have what we desire, instead of crushing ourselves under the weight of our own comparison.

To clear the comparison that can crush us, we have to believe in ourselves and our abilities. We have to move through the resistance that tries to keep us firmly rooted in place.

We have to know that our best work can live inside us for only so long. It needs a place to thrive outside us; it craves a way to support us by becoming an extension of ourselves, not by staying stagnant within.

There's always room at the top; and the top is every level you reach when you do your best work.

And there's always more 'top' to reach, because there's always more work to create and share. I don't say that to make you fear you need to 'hustle' to the top. I say it in the sense that the more you create, the more you can create! Creating gives you confidence, and your confidence helps you create more. It's a magnificent cycle, when you let yourself tap into it.

And oh, you can! You can tap into it by creating your own version of the top, and by looking to the people you admire, and trusting that if there's space for them, there's space for you too. There's space for you and for your work, your message and your voice, because there's always room at the top.

Remember, the top is every level you reach when you do your best work—so go do that.

You're bigger than your work

Every time I write a book, I evolve as a person. I change my mind about things; I open my eyes to other perspectives; I expand what I thought was possible for me; and I connect with the part of me that can't truly explain what it feels like to put fingers to keyboard and let my deepest self come through, in words I don't even know I'll write until I see them in front of me.

There came a time when I was tired of obsessing over how I explained what I did through my work; what labels I gave myself; what I put on my business card. There came a time when I knew I had to step out of defining myself by what I did; that was one piece of me, but not who I was as a whole, and not who I am.

When you put your heart on your sleeve through your creative work and soul work (however it shows up for you), it's all too easy to start thinking of yourself as your business, your work, your writing, your art. However, I've learnt time and time again that while we can put our all into these projects, that doesn't mean we put everything in—we are still separate.

This means that if social media numbers go up or down, you still know you are enough.

If sales aren't as high as you anticipated (or dreamed about), you still know you are enough.

If things don't go the way you planned in your daily planner, you still know you are enough.

If no-one buys your art, gives you the promotion, acknowledges your hard work, says you did a great job, wants to hire you ... you still know you are enough

Your worth doesn't fluctuate with your bank balance. It doesn't fluctuate depending on how many spots you sell in a program, or how often you spoke up in the office today, or how many people want to work with you/hire you/buy your work.

It doesn't fluctuate, because your worth is innate, and there's nothing you can do to change that.

The reverse is also true. You're no more worthy when your bank account is fuller, lusher. You're no more deserving when you sell more spots in a program, or fill an art gallery with people eager to purchase your art, or get a raise or promotion.

The issue is that our ego sometimes gets in the way, and then if things fluctuate, we can believe it's our fault that things haven't gone to plan. We take the lows too personally, because we took the highs too personally.

Perhaps the difference is that when you allow yourself to receive more, that's when you know, trust and honour your worth more, and you communicate this to others as well as to yourself. When you feel more worthy, you have the confidence to speak up, to be seen, to be heard, to show up, step up and take the actions that'll draw in, create, and allow you to receive incredible opportunities, abundance, joy and more.

Maybe if you trusted your enoughness now, you'd make space to call that in. Because you know you are enough, and because you know you're worthy of taking action, and of receiving. That way, you can flow with any fluctuations; you won't take the downs too personally, and you won't take the ups too personally.

Do this by continuing to align your energy, clear away fears, call in what's next, show up, own your gifts, share them with the world, and love what you create.

Okay, this is the end

Thank you for reaching this part; the part where I thank you for being here, for showing up, for making waves in your own life and work, and for honouring yourself, so that you inspire others to honour themselves too.

By reading this book, taking action, clearing your blocks, aligning to what you truly want, and letting yourself receive it (or something better), you're leaps and bounds ahead of where you started (while simultaneously, always being exactly where you need to be).

You're truly and deeply allowing yourself to become aligned and unstoppable, in the best possible way.

It's time to stand in your absolute power, and commit to yourself and your dreams, following your own light—in your own way.

I can't wait to see what you do next*.

So much love,

Cass x

*Or what you don't do. Remember? You're allowed to do stop, drop and chill, whenever you need.

Expand Your Energy Meditation

One more thing before you go ... here is a meditation to clear, balance, align and activate your energy.

Our energy is something we must always choose to look after. Think of it like brushing your teeth or planting a garden. You don't brush your teeth once and think, *Ha, I've done it! I never have to do that again.* Likewise when planting a garden, you may spend a weekend pruning, planting and raking until it looks gorgeous, but in a few weeks you'll want to prune, plant and rake again to maintain what you created.

Similarly, and with lightness, ease and joy, your 'work' with energy balancing is never 'done'; but that doesn't mean it needs to feel like 'work' at all.

Balancing, clearing and aligning your energy is a beautiful thing to do for yourself, and you have full power to do it. That's why I'm offering up the following chakra-balancing, energy-expanding meditation.

Have you heard about chakras before? They're our personal power centres, similar to our physical organs, except that they operate at a much higher frequency. They regulate both physical and subtle energies, so understanding them and looking after them is an important part of living and enjoying a healthy, balanced and aligned life.

The seven main chakras

Base chakra

Located at the base of the spine, it's also called the Root chakra. This chakra is red in colour and relates to your feelings of safety, security and survival in the world, as well as where you fit into your community, and how 'grounded' you feel. The organs it relates to are the adrenal glands. If this chakra is unbalanced, you may feel ungrounded, fearful, and unsure of your place in the world. When it's balanced, you'll feel grounded, safe, secure and deeply rooted in your life and within yourself.

Sacral chakra

Located near your navel, this chakra is orange in colour and relates to your sexuality, creativity, ability to create, and ability to relate to others in relationships and in your own body. The organs related to this chakra are the reproductive organs, including the womb. If this chakra is unbalanced, you may feel sexually and creatively blocked, and suffer from reproductive issues such as PMS or lack of periods. You may find it hard to maintain relationships or feel creative or fertile—in any sense of the word—in your life. On the flip side, when it's clear and balanced, your creativity will flow, your male/female sides of self will feel balanced too (doing vs. being), and you'll have clear, firm and healthy boundaries within yourself and towards others.

Solar Plexus chakra

Located between the navel and the base of your sternum (think stomach area), this chakra is yellow in colour and relates to your feelings of self: self-confidence, self-trust, self-worth, self-esteem and inner power. Physically, it relates to the pancreas. If this chakra is unbalanced, you may feel insecure, powerless, lacking in self-worth and confidence, and unworthy. You may also be sabotaging yourself or an area of your life. When it's cleansed and balanced, you'll feel confident, powerful, self-assured in your personal identity, keen to take action on your goals and what brings you joy, and you'll deeply trust yourself too. You'll know you are enough.

Heart chakra

Located in the centre of the chest, this chakra is green in colour and relates to your feelings and emotions in relation to yourself and others, to giving and receiving love and forgiveness, and to gratitude and appreciation. Its mission is relationships and healing. It relates to the heart, circulatory system and breasts. If this chakra is unbalanced, you may find it hard to love and forgive yourself and others, to be compassionate to yourself and others, or to feel gratitude in your life. When this chakra is balanced, you'll easily give and receive love (to both yourself and others), you'll be compassionate towards yourself and others, you'll be able to forgive yourself and others, and you'll be able to let go of guilt.

Throat chakra

Located in the throat area, this blue chakra relates to communication and expression (to self and others), truth, speaking up and self-responsibility. It relates to the thyroid. When this chakra is unbalanced, you may find it hard to communicate, to express yourself and speak up, and you may often get a sore throat. When it's balanced, you'll easily listen to your own needs and speak up about your truth (expressing it to others too), you'll be able to ask for what you need, and you'll hear and feel heard by others.

Brow chakra

Located between the eyes, this purple/indigo chakra, relates to vision, intuition, insight, hindsight and future sight. It relates to the pituitary glands and eyes. If this chakra is unbalanced, it may be hard for you to tap into your intuition or you may feel a block around this, as well as finding it hard to look ahead or look within. When balanced, you'll have a clear sense of your intuition and bigger vision. You'll trust your intuition, you'll firmly make decisions, and you'll clearly see what to do next.

Crown chakra

Located at the top of the head, this white chakra relates to your spiritual nature, and your connection with the Divine, with the Universe, and with your Higher Self. It relates to your purpose and spirituality; physically, it relates to the pineal gland. If this chakra is blocked or unbalanced, you may find it hard to tap into source energy, to feel abundant, to feel connected to the Divine, the Universe, or to something greater than yourself; you may feel lost, spiritually and in your life, as if you've lost your soul purpose. When this chakra is balanced and clear, you'll feel connected to and supported by something higher and greater, you'll feel connected to the flow and abundance of life, and you'll find yourself able to receive guidance and support from the Universe, a higher power, or whatever you believe in.

Now that you understand a little more about these powerful energy centres, you can see how important it is that we keep them cleansed, aligned and balanced. There are many ways to balance the chakras: you can use sound, essential oils, yoga, kinesiology, reiki and, of course, meditation.

How to use this meditation

You can use the following meditation script in any way you wish. You can read it slowly in one go. You can read it paragraph by paragraph, closing your eyes in between each one, to let the words and energy wash over you and through you. You can record yourself speaking it, then listen back like a guided meditation. It's your choice.

Its purpose

The purpose of this meditation is to help you expand the energy of your creativity, work, and business, as well as your self-expression and self-belief, so you can shift out of a space of feeling small, stuck or invisible, and align yourself to what you wish to call in next.

When we align to the energies of expansion, we draw abundance towards us and into our lives and work; we allow ourselves to receive (more money, more visibility, more opportunities, more clients, or more of whatever we're working towards). We find our flow, and carve a path that's deeply aligned to who we are.

This meditation is perfect for you if you've been feeling a little 'left behind' in your endeavours; if you're feeling swamped or overwhelmed; if you've been comparing yourself to others, feeling lost or confused, not sure how (or when) to move forwards; and if you're tired of being on the creative roller-coaster.

As we begin, give yourself permission to let go of where you think you should be; let go of what you think you've done wrong, or not enough of; let go of your ego's chitchat that may be putting other people on pedestals. Let go, let go, let go.

Allow yourself to be here now, to give yourself—and the energy of your creativity, your business, your work, your path—what is needed. Allow yourself to receive, to uplevel, to expand, to persevere. Allow yourself to succeed in your own way.

During this meditation, if you need to cry, or shift your body, or shake (or shimmy!), or place your hands over certain areas of your body to help release and clear energy, please do so.

Okay, let's begin

I invite you to place your hands over your heart, take a deep breath in and out, and settle into this very moment, here and now.

Take your attention to your Base chakra, at the base of your spine, and see beautiful red smoke swirl through your lower back, your hips, your legs, and down to your feet.

See this red smoke becoming deeper and denser where you may be holding onto fears, tension or tightness. See it being absorbed by your body where you need it most. In doing so, feel and sense it helping to lighten the load for you, healing any energy leaks, helping to absorb your fears, helping you ground into yourself, into the energy of your business or work, into your community and tribe.

Sense it burning away like fire, helping to transmute and transform the blocks that are keeping you from feeling grounded and safe, the fears that may be holding you back, the limiting beliefs or attitudes you may be carrying.

Sense this red smoke swirling through your base, expanding it, grounding it, recalibrating your energy. Sense this smoke allowing you to stand firm on your ground, allowing you to grow roots, to expand, to move your life, business or work forwards, while anchoring you into yourself.

See this red smoke bring you any messages or insights you need most right now.

Now see this smoke move upwards, to your lower abdomen, your Sacral chakra. See it transform into orange as it swirls through, picking up and absorbing any tendencies you've been carrying to push or force, any imbalances in your ability to take action and receive, to do and to be.

Allow this orange smoke to flow in and out of you, envisioning it helping to clean up what's no longer needed, transforming and transmuting it, healing any energy leaks, re-energising you, and allowing you to feel in tune with yourself, your creativity, and your flow.

Allow this orange smoke to bring you any other messages or insights you need most right now.

Now see this smoke shift upwards to your upper stomach area, your Solar Plexus chakra, transforming into a vibrant yellow. This yellow smoke swirls in and out, around and through you, picking up any feelings of not being enough, any fears you may hold about your power, and any feelings of comparison or lack of self-belief.

In the place of all of that, this yellow smoke infuses energy, vitality, confidence, self-esteem, self-belief and a deep and unwavering sense of personal power. The yellow smoke helps you see that you are enough, that your creativity is enough, your voice is enough, your work is enough, and it asks you to believe this, to live this truth.

This yellow smoke helps to shift your energy from that of a victim, to that of a leader. You are ready for what is next; you are enough.

Allow this yellow smoke to bring you any other messages or insights you need most right now.

This smoke moves upwards again, to your chest area, your Heart chakra. It's turned green in colour, and is helping to integrate and connect your entire energy system. This green smoke is helping to dissolve pain, fear, regret, shame, guilt, anger and rage, as well as feelings of emptiness, burnout and disconnection.

This green smoke is helping you connect with the energy of your creativity and your work, on an even deeper level. It's helping you connect with your clients and customers, with the work you want to be doing in the world, with the way you want to be showing up, and with how you want to be connecting with others.

This green smoke is helping you accept where you are today. It's transmuting anger or fear into love and compassion.

This green smoke now swirls around the centre of your chest, in and around your heart. Let your heart pump this green energy, this healing green vitality through your entire body—into every cell, every organ, every vein and artery, every inch of you. This green smoke is connecting you to your highest potential, by allowing you to love, accept, forgive and receive, and to give and connect from that place.

Now breathe it into your lungs, your chest rising with each inhalation, and falling with each exhalation. Allow yourself to breathe out this healing green energy to allow it to reach your amazing business or work community, to allow it to draw abundance, visibility, opportunities and clients towards you.

Allow this green smoke to bring you any messages or insights you need most right now.

See this green smoke move upwards again to your throat area, your Throat chakra. See it turn blue in colour, as it absorbs any blocks to communicating what you do and how you help people, to speaking up about yourself and your work, to using your voice as an empowering tool.

Allow this blue smoke to pick up what you no longer need, and see these blocks being dissolved and then dissipating. This allows you to make the rights choices for you, to speak up and allow yourself to be heard, to listen to others, to yourself, and to your Higher Self and Guides.

Allow this blue smoke to bring you any messages or insights you need most right now.

See this smoke as it moves upwards once more, towards your Third Eye chakra in the centre of your forehead, turning indigo. It clears and cleanses your perceptions of where you are, to allow you to see and perceive your situation with less judgement, and with more compassion and love.

This indigo smoke swirls through you, clearing away any fog that may have been obscuring your intuition, your inner vision, your ability to manifest and envision what you desire. It helps clear the way for you to move forwards, in deeper alignment with your inner guide and your intuition.

It helps to transmute and transform overthinking, or any fears that are holding you back, into simplicity and courage. It allows you to see the bigger picture, to invite in more clarity, and to feel clearer about your path in your life, creativity and work.

Allow this indigo smoke to bring you any messages or insights you need most right now.

This indigo smoke now shifts upwards one more time to your Crown chakra, located at the top of your head. The smoke turns to an iridescent white-gold colour, clearing and balancing the energy of your Crown chakra.

This allows you to fully trust where you are, to invite in guidance from your Guides and the Universe, to allow you to feel deeply supported on your path.

This white-gold smoke re-energises your entire chakra and energy system, filling every cell in your body with energy, trust, clarity, divine guidance and support. You allow abundance in, because you trust in its cycle; you trust that there is always more where that came from.

Allow this white-gold smoke to bring you any messages or insights you need most right now.

Take a deep breath in and out. Take your focus to just outside your body. See yourself surrounded by a golden, white light. See yourself protected, supported and energised. See yourself exactly where you are today, not in the past, and not in the future. Let yourself be here, today.

Give yourself permission to expand your energy to hold more space for what you're calling in. Trust that you can not only expand with grace, but that you can hold space for more clients, more customers, more visibility, more abundance, more cash flow and more money, as well as more joy, ease, freedom and flow in your life and work.

Deeply allow yourself to let go of fears of lack and failure, to allow yourself to move forwards. Thank yourself, your creativity and your work for where you've been, for where you are, and for where you're going.

Now that the seven colours of smoke have cleared, balanced and aligned your energy, allow them to merge into a deep swirl of technicolour smoke. Allow this technicolour smoke to continue to swirl up and down, around you, through you, over and under you. See it moving through you as you uplevel your energy, to allow yourself to open up to receive.

See this smoke swirl around you, as you allow yourself to feel more optimistic about your path ahead.

See this smoke trailing behind you, as you envision yourself walking away from whatever is making you feel stuck, blocked or small.

See this smoke grounding down below your feet, as you ground into your body and the energy of your creativity and work, to help you draw your dreams and goals (or something better) towards you.

See this smoke as you take steps forwards, feeling supported, grounded and in alignment, as you continue to expand in a way that feels right for you.

Now take a moment to thank the healing and balancing energies of this smoke that has supported you through—and will support you beyond—this meditation. Remember you can call upon it at any time, to help shift, clear, balance and align your energy.

Take a few deep breaths in and out now, coming back into this space and time, and open your eyes when you're ready.

Bibliography

The following books, websites and resources were referred to throughout the writing of this book:

Big Magic, Elizabeth Gilbert

Brave Enough, Cheryl Strayed

Floral Acupuncture, Deborah Craydon, C.F.E.P. and Warren Bellows, LIC.AC.

Herbs and Natural Supplements, 3rd ed, Lesley Braun and Marc Cohen

Herding Tigers, Todd Henry

How to Sit, Thich Nhat Hanh

Liquid Crystal Oracle Guidebook, Justin Moikeha Asar

Principles and Practices of Phytotherapy, 2nd ed, Kerry Bone and Simon Mills

The Bach Centre: https://www.bachcentre.com/index.php

The Subtle Body Practice Manual: A Comprehensive Guide to Energy Healing, Cyndi Dale

The War of Art, Steven Pressfield

Stay in Touch

I'd love for us to stay in touch. For more support in trusting yourself, your creativity, and your path in life and business, visit my website at www.cassiemendozajones.com to learn more about my books, private coaching, online courses, programs, events, meditations, articles, free resources and more.

You'll also find me on social media:
Instagram.com/cassiemendozajones
Facebook.com/cassiemendozajones
Pinterest.com/cmendozajones
Twitter.com/cmendozajones

#AlignedAndUnstoppableBook

Acknowledgements

A huge thank you to ...

The team at Hay House: Thank you for believing in me again, and for allowing this book to come to fruition in its own time. I wish I could tell younger (nervous!) Cass that, on walking into your office all those years ago, she'd be standing here today, saying 'thank you' for publishing a third book. What a wonderful ride it's been so far.

Edie Swan: Thank you for designing such a perfect cover. It is all the things I wanted it to be—energising, calming, magnetic and more. Working with you was a dream.

To my readers: Thank you for reading my words, and for telling me they help your heart. It means the world to me, and I will never, ever get tired of seeing my books in your hands.

To my clients: Thank you for sharing your stories so openly, for allowing me to share them here, and for teaching me more than you know.

To my loves, Nic and Asher: Thank you for lighting up my life. You are the best reasons I can think of to inspire me to become more deeply aligned and unstoppable.

About the Author

Cassie Mendoza-Jones is the bestselling author of *You Are Enough, It's All Good* and *Aligned and Unstoppable* (Hay House). She is also a kinesiologist, business alignment coach, naturopath, writer and speaker.

Cassie works with women, and with entrepreneurs, healers, coaches and creatives who are driven and devoted to honouring their dreams, and who want to become more powerfully aligned to their bigger vision, clear away perfectionism, procrastination and overwhelm, and create their own version of a beautiful and aligned business and life.

With a soft spot for fellow perfectionists and a focus on energy and emotions, Cassie uses a combination of kinesiology, business alignment coaching and a touch of naturopathy to support women in getting clear on their next steps, uplevelling their mindsets, and increasing their clarity, confidence and energy, so they can create thriving lives and businesses.

Her work is for you, if you're ready to let go of limiting beliefs, fears and worrying thoughts that consume you, and if you want to build a life and business that feels really good to you.

Her lessons and insights have been featured on live national TV on *Today Extra*; in national and international publications such as *Collective Hub*, *body+soul*, *Women's Fitness* and *Australian Natural Health*; and on popular websites such as ELLE, The Daily Guru, news.com.au, Vogue.com.au, Sporteluxe, marie claire and smh.com.au. She's been interviewed on countless podcasts, and spoken at events and workshops around Australia for a variety of companies, such as BUPA, Barre Body, New Balance, LinkedIn, Morgan Stanley, Mirvac and Eat Fit Food, as well as for her own popular workshops, book tours, and events.

When she's not working, you can find her taking her little girl Asher for a walk, drinking all the coffee with her hubby, Nic, getting lost in a good novel, making another cup of tea, deciding if she should buy more scatter cushions for the couch (she shouldn't), or suiting up for a yoga class.

Meet Cassie and align to more freedom and harmony in your life and business at: **www.cassiemendozajones.com**

We hope you enjoyed this Hay House book. If you'd like to receive our online catalog featuring additional information on Hay House books and products, or if you'd like to find out more about the Hay Foundation, please contact:

Hay House, Inc., P.O. Box 5100, Carlsbad, CA 92018-5100
(760) 431-7695 or (800) 654-5126
(760) 431-6948 (fax) or (800) 650-5115 (fax)
www.hayhouse.com® • www.hayfoundation.org

———

Published in Australia by: Hay House Australia Pty. Ltd.,
18/36 Ralph St., Alexandria NSW 2015
Phone: 612-9669-4299 • *Fax:* 612-9669-4144
www.hayhouse.com.au

Published in the United Kingdom by: Hay House UK, Ltd.,
The Sixth Floor, Watson House, 54 Baker Street, London W1U 7BU
Phone: +44 (0)20 3927 7290 • *Fax:* +44 (0)20 3927 7291
www.hayhouse.co.uk

Published in India by: Hay House Publishers India,
Muskaan Complex, Plot No. 3, B-2, Vasant Kunj, New Delhi 110 070
Phone: 91-11-4176-1620 • *Fax:* 91-11-4176-1630
www.hayhouse.co.in

———

Access New Knowledge.
Anytime. Anywhere.

Learn and evolve at your own pace
with the world's leading experts.

www.hayhouseU.com